Words for Students of English

Vocabulary Series Editors
Holly Deemer Rogerson
Lionel Menasche

Meikle
Blossom

WORDS
for Students of English

A Vocabulary Series for ESL

Holly Deemer Rogerson
Suzanne T. Hershelman
Carol Jasnow
Carol Moltz

University of Pittsburgh Press for the English Language Institute
of the University of Pittsburgh

Pitt Series in English as a Second Language

Distributed by the University of Pittsburgh Press,
127 N. Bellefield Ave., Pittsburgh, Pa. 15260

Illustrations by Suzanne T. Hershelman

Contents

Foreword

The objective of this series of vocabulary texts for the student of English as a foreign language is to facilitate the learning of approximately 3,000 new base words. Vocabulary learning has long been deemphasized in language teaching, much to the detriment of the students, who have mostly been left to fend for themselves. We thoroughly agree with Muriel Saville-Troike, who states, "Vocabulary knowledge in English is the most important aspect of oral English proficiency for academic achievement" (*TESOL Quarterly*, vol. 18, no. 2, p. 216).

With the present lack of comprehensive vocabulary texts suitable for both classroom use and home study, this series is intended to support teachers in preparing effective vocabulary lessons so that they can meet their students' urgent need for an increased lexicon. We present here a selection of base vocabulary items and some of their derived forms (i.e., the noun, verb, adverb, and adjective of the same stem) together with a series of exercises designed to help students remember the new words and use them in context.

This text has been used in an experimental edition in the English Language Institute, and modifications suggested by its use have been incorporated in the present version.

Christina Bratt Paulston
Director, English Language Institute
University of Pittsburgh

Acknowledgments

A series such as this depends greatly on the cooperation and hard work of numerous people:

Christina Bratt Paulston and Holly Deemer Rogerson originated the idea for the series.

Christina Bratt Paulston provided ongoing support for the series.

Mary Newton Bruder, Carol Jasnow, Christina Bratt Paulston, and Holly Deemer Rogerson developed the first version of the list of approximately 600 words assumed known.

Holly Deemer Rogerson developed the original pool of words from which the 150 topic word lists were chosen. She also organized the word lists and provided general management of the project, including authors' drafts, revisions, editing, illustrations, duplicating, testing, and typing.

Ideas for word lists, format, and exercise types were contributed by Betsy Davis, Gary Esarey, Suzanne T. Hershelman, Carol Jasnow, Carol Moltz, Lionel Menasche, Holly Deemer Rogerson, Dorolyn Smith, and Linda M. Schmandt.

Final revisions of content were done by Lionel Menasche and Holly Deemer Rogerson, with input from classroom testing by Isabel Dillener, Caroline Haessly, Pat Furey, Carol Jasnow, Linda M. Schmandt, Jill Sherman, and Tom Swinscoe.

JoEllen Walker typed several drafts of the manuscript.

Lisa Krizmanich assisted during the testing phase.

Introduction

Volumes 1–6 of *Words for Students of English*, each containing 25 units, present English base words,* with definitions, examples, and exercises. The texts may be used as core texts for vocabulary learning classes or as supplementary texts in reading, speaking, and writing classes. They may also be used for individual study.

Each unit focuses on one topic so that the words being presented can be practiced in meaningful contexts. Some of the new words in each unit are directly related to the topic, while others are less directly connected. Most of the words in a given unit can be used in a variety of contexts.

Volume 1 assumes a knowledge of 600 base words in English. Starting from this point, new words are presented in each unit, with the definitions, examples, and exercises *containing only vocabulary which has been previously learned.* The first units in Volume 1 contain only about ten base words each in order to allow the students to become familiar with the format of the units. After the first units, each unit in Volume 1 contains approximately fifteen base words. In Volume 2, there are approximately fifteen base words in each unit. In Volumes 3 and 4, each unit contains fifteen to twenty base words, and, in Volumes 5 and 6, there are approximately 25 base words per unit. On completion of the series of six volumes, students will have learned approximately 3,000 base words.

Given that Volume 1 assumes a knowledge of 600 base words, the level of Volumes 1 and 2 can be loosely described as beginning, Volumes 3 and 4 as intermediate, and Volumes 5 and 6 as high intermediate or advanced.

---

*"Base" may be defined variously in lexical analysis, but for our present pedagogical purpose it implies any alternant from which other forms are derived. It is frequently impossible to say which form of a word is the most basic.

Selection of Words and Unit Topics

The 600 assumed words upon which Volumes 1–6 are based were chosen by a panel of experienced ESL teachers at the University of Pittsburgh as the group of words which are most typically learned by ESL students during their first two years of middle school or high school ESL classes. The words presented in Volumes 1–6 were selected according to usefulness from a variety of word-frequency lists. The authors and editors added other words to the topics at suitable levels of difficulty.

In many cases students have to learn words with more than one meaning or with meanings that may vary according to context. A decision was made in each such instance as to whether the meaning in the new context was different enough to warrant further definition or similar enough for the students to extrapolate from what they had previously learned. These decisions were based on dictionary definitions and authors' or editors' personal judgments. For example, a word such as *beat* might appear in these contexts: (a) beat the opposing football team, (b) beat a drum, (c) a beat of a heart, (d) beat a person. Contexts (b) and (d) (meaning = strike) were judged close enough to allow extrapolation of meaning from one context to another, but (a) and (c) were thought to require separate definitions.

We have assumed that when a student learns a new vocabulary item, an approximate meaning for the word is assimilated, and that meaning is linked to the context in which the word was first encountered. Then, as the student meets the word in other contexts, the initially learned, approximate meaning is expanded and refined. Hence, many words are not only used several times in the unit in which they first appear, but are also used in later units.

The unit topics were chosen and ordered according to their perceived relevance to the students' lives, that is, their communicative usefulness. Most topics are covered in one unit in each volume, but certain broad topics, for example "School," are repeated twice within the same volume, in which case they are marked (A) or (B). A few topics, such as "Religion" and "Banking," due to the difficulty or abstractness of the words associated with them, are not covered in the first volume. Certain other topics whose words were perceived as tangible and easy, for example, "Telephone" and "Post Office," are completed in the first two volumes.

It should be noted that the repetition of each topic, at times within the same volume and always in at least one subsequent volume, allows for review and recycling of the material learned. Thus, long-term retention of the vocabulary is facilitated.

Format and Suggestions for Teachers

Flexibility in using this vocabulary series has been a prime consideration in planning the format and exercises of the units. Therefore, although suggestions are given in the following paragraphs, it is assumed that teachers in different situations will decide according to their own students' needs whether work should be done in or out of class, orally or in writing, and with or without direct assistance from the teacher. The pace at which classes can proceed through each volume will vary greatly, depending on the students' motivation, study habits, and general workload, as well as the degree of emphasis the teacher wishes to place on productive vocabulary skills.

Each unit in Volumes 1–6 has the same format. The five sections of each unit are as follows.

WORD FORM CHART
DEFINITIONS AND EXAMPLES
INTRODUCTORY EXERCISES
STUDY EXERCISES
FOLLOW-UP

The WORD FORM CHART presents base words and some or all of their related forms, categorized by part of speech. In Volumes 1 and 2, an effort was made to simplify the charts by omitting many derived or related forms which were either not common, or not useful for students at this level, or not easily recognizable from a knowledge of the base form. After Volume 2, more related forms are added because the students can handle more as they progress in learning the language. Decisions on what forms to omit were made by authors and editors on the basis of experience gained during testing of these materials with linguistically heterogeneous classes. Teachers in different educational contexts should consider supplementing the charts according to their own students' needs and their ability to absorb more material. For example, many words could be added by giving antonyms formed from words already given (planned/unplanned, honest/dishonest).

In the NOUNS column of the charts in Volumes 1 and 2 only, nouns which normally or frequently refer to humans are marked by the symbol ⚥. When a noun, as defined in the unit, can be either human or nonhuman, the symbol is in parentheses: (⚥). Gerunds are not included in the charts. Nouns have not been marked "count" and "non-count" because so many nouns function in both ways.

In the VERBS column, irregular past tenses and past participles are in parentheses following the verbs. In cases where more than one past tense or past participle is acceptable, the more regular one is included in the chart. Thus, for example, in the Volume 1, Unit #4 Word Form Chart no irregular forms are listed for *forecast* because the regular form *forecasted* is also currently acceptable.

In the ADJECTIVES column, we have included any present or past participles that appear prenominally as adjectives, as well as any regular adjectives. We have not included in this column nouns which form Noun-Noun modification patterns.

The next section, DEFINITIONS AND EXAMPLES, gives the meanings of the words as well as example sentences which are usually related to the topic of the unit. The form chosen for definition is not always the base form. Other forms are sometimes chosen for greater ease of definition or learning. In all definitions and examples, only previously learned words are used. This applies also within the set of definitions in each unit. Thus, the words in each set of definitions are presented in an order which allows their definition and exemplification using only previously introduced words. Grammatical information is given in the definitions by means of the following conventions: "to" is used before a verb to indicate the verb form, articles are used with nouns whenever possible to indicate that the word is a noun, and parentheses enclose prepositions that may follow a verb. Words with more than one meaning are cross-referenced to definitions in earlier units when new definitions are given. This section, together with the Word Form Chart, can be efficiently handled as work assigned for intensive individual study, followed by discussion in class of questions raised by students. At this point the teacher may also wish to elaborate on certain definitions and give further examples.

Writing explicit definitions of words using the intentionally limited vocabulary available results in some rather broad definitions and others that are limited to certain aspects of the meaning. The deliberate compromise here between precision and generality is designed to make the text fully accessible to students by avoiding the major weakness of many other vocabulary texts: defining new items with words that are themselves unknown to the learner. The easily understood broad definitions, which may take the form of a standard verbal definition, a picture, or a list of examples, are then refined by further exposure to appropriate examples in this unit and series and in the students' later reading. Also, students can usefully refer to a bilingual dictionary in conjunction with studying the example sentences given.

After the Definitions and Examples section, there is a three-tiered system of exercises sequenced to take the student from easy, open-book, fairly controlled exercises through more difficult, less controlled exercises to a final phase with communicative exercises.

The first part of the sequence consists of INTRODUCTORY EXERCISES. These are designed to acquaint the students with the new words in the unit and lead them to an initial understanding of the words by using the Definitions and Examples section. We recommend that these brief and easy exercises be done with books open, orally or in writing, immediately after the teacher's first presentation of the new words.

The next section in each unit, headed STUDY EXERCISES, is a longer and more difficult set of exercises designed to be used by the students for individual study or for oral or written work in class.

The final section is the FOLLOW-UP. This includes a dictation and more open-ended communicative exercises designed to be done after the students have studied the words. The latter may be done orally in class, or teachers may request written answers to selected questions.

Each volume also contains an INDEX listing all the base words presented in that volume. Words in the preceding volumes are given in separate appendices. With each word is listed the volume and unit where it is presented. The 600 initially assumed words are also in an appendix.

An ANSWER KEY at the end of each volume provides answers for all the exercises in the Study Exercises sections, except where a variety of answers is acceptable. Answers are not provided for the Introductory Exercises or the exercises in the Follow-Up so that the teacher can choose to use these exercises for homework or testing purposes if desired.

Production and Recognition

Although a distinction between vocabulary known for recognition and that known for production is often propounded, the actual situation is probably best represented by a continuum stretching from mere recognition to production which is accurate both semantically and syntactically. The exercises in Volumes 1–6 cover the full range of this continuum so that teachers wishing to stress productive vocabulary knowledge will have ample opportunity to give their students feedback on the use of the new words in their speech and writing. However, the goal of many teachers will be to increase their students' recognition vocabularies as rapidly as possible, with the expectation that those words which students meet again frequently in other contexts and have a use for will gradually become part of their productive vocabularies. Teachers with this goal of recognition vocabulary development in mind will wish to proceed more rapidly through the units and deemphasize those exercises requiring productive capabilities, for example, by limiting their corrections to semantic errors, rather than correcting syntactic mistakes as well.

Words for Students of English

Education (A)

Word Form Chart

NOUN	VERB	ADJECTIVE	ADVERB	CONJUNCTION
admission	admit	admitted		
			almost	
attention	attend	attentive	attentively	
average	average	average		
				however
instructor	instruct	instructive	instructively	
instruction		instructional	instructionally	
lecture	lecture			
lecturer				
literature		literary		
necessity	necessitate	necessary	necessarily	
novel				
novelist				
poem		poetic	poetically	
poet				
poetry				
praise	praise	praiseworthy		
review	review			
rule	rule	ruling		
ruler				
seminar				

Definitions and Examples

1. **admit** [to allow to enter]

    Fred was **admitted** to an engineering college.

    A: What is the price of **admission** to the basketball game?
    B: About five dollars.

2. **almost** [not completely]

    My sister is **almost** twelve years old. She will be twelve next month.

    A: Are you **almost** finished painting?
    B: Yes. I'll be finished soon.

3. **attention** [careful watching or listening]

    A sick baby needs medical **attention**.

    A: Please pay **attention**. This information is important.
    B: OK. I'm listening.

4. **average** [the usual type or number; typical]

    The **average** family in the United States does not have any servants.
    The **average** of three, four, and eight is five. $(3 + 4 + 8) \div 3 = 5$

    A: What is the **average** temperature in the summer?
    B: About 80 degrees Fahrenheit.

5. **however** [but]

    He is a handsome young man. **However**, his personality is not very pleasant.
    We planned a class picnic; **however**, it rained all weekend and we did not go.

6. **instruct** [to teach; to show how to do or use something]

    Read the **instructions** before you use the electric typewriter.

    A: Who is the biology **instructor**?
    B: Dr. Fisher, I think.

7. **lecture** [a talk given to an audience]

    This **lecture** hall has comfortable chairs.

    A: Did you hear the **lecture** on air pollution?
    B: Yes. I learned a lot about the environment.

8. **necessary** [needed; required]

    Food and water are **necessary** for life.

    A: How many people are **necessary** to make a basketball team?
    B: Five.

9. **novel** [a long written story about people who are invented by the author]

    Most famous **novelists** write about one or two favorite subjects.

    A: What did you do on your vacation at the beach?
    B: It rained, so I stayed indoors and read three **novels**.

10. **poem** [a type of writing that often tells about strong feelings and is written in beautiful and musical language]

    Few **poets** earn a sufficient salary.

    A: Have you published your **poem**?
    B: No. The magazine returned it to me.

11. **literature** [the books and writings of a country, subject, or time]

    My roommate is studying American **literature**.

    A: Is this **literature** course required?
    B: Yes. It's compulsory.

12. **praise** [to speak well of a thing or person]

    The boss **praises** his employees when they work long hours.

    A: Why did you give Ted so much **praise**?
    B: Because he's so cooperative.

13. **review** [to study or look at again]

    You should **review** lesson six before the test.

    A: Have you **reviewed** your plan for tomorrow?
    B: Yes. Some changes are necessary.

14. **rule** [a law; what you can and cannot do]

    There are many **rules** governing dormitory living.

    A: Did you win the game?
    B: No. I forgot the **rules**.

15. **seminar** [a small class where the students are often required to give information and talk about it]

    Advanced students often go to **seminars**.

    A: When does the **seminar** meet?
    B: Every Wednesday at 10:00.

Introductory Exercises

A. Match each word with its definition.

____ **1.** not completely		**a.** admit
____ **2.** to teach		**b.** almost
____ **3.** required		**c.** average
____ **4.** to allow to enter		**d.** however
____ **5.** typical		**e.** instruct
____ **6.** but		**f.** lecture
____ **7.** a law		**g.** literature
____ **8.** to study again		**h.** necessary
____ **9.** a small class		**i.** review
		j. rule
		k. seminar

B. Answer each question with a word from the word form chart in this unit.

1. What type of writing is written in beautiful and musical language?
2. What is a talk given to an audience?
3. What should you do before a test?
4. Who lectures to the class?
5. What do you need to know before you play a game?
6. Who writes poetry?
7. What are the books and writings about a subject?
8. What is a small class for advanced students?
9. What does a boss give to good employees?
10. How should you listen to a lecture?

Study Exercises

C. Write **T** if the sentence is true and **F** if it is false.

____ **1.** Novelists write poetry.

____ **2.** Seminars are usually small classes.

____ **3.** You should pay attention to your instructor.

____ **4.** Teachers praise the bad students.

____ **5.** The best high school students are usually admitted to college.

____ **6.** The average student does perfect homework.

_____ 7. Music and dance are part of literature.

_____ 8. In a literature class it is necessary to read many things.

_____ 9. You should review all of the lectures before a test.

D. In the blanks, write the appropriate word(s) from the word form chart in this unit.

1. A poetry course is required for graduation; _____ , no literature course is given in the summer.

2. A child should pay _____ when his parents speak.

3. Do you like to read _____-s ? No. I prefer poetry, plays, and short stories.

4. An instructor usually _____-s students who study a lot.

5. I'm hungry. It's _____ time for lunch.

6. A famous professor will _____ tomorrow about biological engineering.

7. This school has too many _____-s, and students often complain that they don't have any freedom.

8. A group of students planned a(n) _____ on the night before the test.

E. Write sentences with the words.

1. good / receives / a / praise / student

_____

2. review / please / rules / grammar / the

_____

3. meets / the / at 9:00 / seminar

_____

4. is necessary / health / exercise / good / for

_____

5. to / teacher / attention / the / pay

_____

F. Read the passage and answer the true or false questions that follow.

After high school, Martha was admitted to a good
university. She expects to major in chemical engineering, but
a literature course is compulsory for all undergraduate
students.

5 Martha is an average student but not a lazy one. She
enjoyed the lectures about poetry during the first weeks of
the course. She was rarely absent and received good grades.

However, during the last part of the course, the class
read novels. She found the books boring and had difficulty
10 paying attention to the seminar, and she failed to complete
some of the necessary assignments.

Martha is finished with literature now. She passed the
course but is happier in engineering.

_____ **1.** Martha is an engineering student.

_____ **2.** She likes to read poetry.

_____ **3.** She is an average student.

_____ **4.** She likes to read novels.

_____ **5.** She often slept in class.

_____ **6.** She completed all of the assignments.

_____ **7.** She is a literature student now.

Follow-up

G. Dictation: Write the sentences that your teacher reads aloud.

1. _____

2. _____

3. _____

4. _____

5. _____

H. Answer the following questions.

1. How many students are admitted to the best university in your country?
2. How many children are in the average family in your country?
3. What is the name of a famous poet or novelist from your country?
4. Do you know the rules for a card game? Explain some of them.
5. Are university instructors respected in your country?
6. Do students in your country prefer literature or engineering?
7. How large are the lecture classes at universities in your country?
8. What is necessary for admission to a university in your country?
9. When do you pay attention in a class?
10. How do you review new vocabulary?

I. Describe a school where you have studied.

1. What courses were given there?
2. What courses did you take?
3. Describe one of the instructors.

Work (A)

Word Form Chart

NOUN	VERB	ADJECTIVE	ADVERB
accomplishment	accomplish	accomplished	
argument	argue	arguable	arguably
		argumentative	argumentatively
			at once
complication	complicate	complicated	
description	describe	descriptive	descriptively
executive	execute	executive	
increase	increase	increased	
		increasing	increasingly
labor	labor	laborious	laboriously
laborer			
manufacture	manufacture	manufactured	
manufacturing		manufacturing	
manufacturer			
negotiation			
negotiator	negotiate	negotiable	
occupation		occupational	
offer	offer		
staff	staff		
state			
stress	stress	stressful	

Definitions and Examples

1. **at once** [as soon as possible; now]

    Our office must do all this work **at once**.
    The boss wants this plan finished **at once**; he will give us no more
    time.

2. **argument** (a) [a fight with words; an opposite idea]

    Our boss had a big **argument** with the president of another
    company about how much money to pay for certain products.
    Jim is very **argumentative**.

    (b) [a strong reason]

    She had no **arguments** to prove her idea.

3. **describe** [to give an idea of something by using spoken or written
    words]

    The president **described** very carefully how his company works.
    I **described** my old job for him so that he would know what kind of
    experience I had had.

4. **manufacture** [to make in a factory]

    Our city **manufactures** shoes and other leather products as well as
    all types of clothing.
    This company **manufactures** computers and similar products.

5. **staff** [all the people who work in a company, school, business, etc.]

    The **staff** is really happy about receiving a raise in salary.
    The boss never has any problems with his **staff**.

6. **increase** [to grow in size, number, etc.; to make larger]

    He **increased** our salaries by ten percent.
    Business has **increased** greatly this year; people are buying more
    than last year.
    The president **increased** the size of our staff from 26 to 36 people.

7. **executive** [a person responsible for managing a business]

    Mrs. Smith is the head **executive** of our company; she makes all the
    final decisions.
    We have several **executives** who work together in planning the
    direction of the company.

8. **complicated** [difficult; difficult to understand]

   The staff have some very **complicated** jobs to complete.
   Manufacturing is a **complicated** activity; there are a lot of things to take care of.

9. **accomplish** [to succeed in finishing something]

   He **accomplished** a lot of work today.
   Suzanne **accomplished** her plan by getting help from many people.

10. **occupation** [a job; a profession]

    My sister is going to change **occupations**; she is tired of working in the business world.

    A: What is his **occupation**?
    B: He is the president of his own company.

11. **offer** [to present something which can be accepted or not]

    Molly **offered** many good ideas to increase production.
    John **offered** to work late to help finish the job.
    He did not accept the salary **offer** I made; he wanted more money.

12. **labor** [the work done or the effort made; the work done for hire in production]

    A lot of **labor** went into manufacturing those cars.
    Increases in **labor** costs caused the company to close.

13. **stressful** [causing worry]

    They had a **stressful** meeting; all the members were arguing about everything.
    It was **stressful** to know that she had a lot to do in such a short time.

14. **state** [condition]

    His business is in a terrible **state**; he is losing thousands of dollars a week.
    She is so nervous! I've never seen her in such a **state**.

15. **negotiate** [to talk together until the people, companies, etc., get what they want]

    They **negotiated** until each company was satisfied with the price.
    The staff must **negotiate** a new salary contract each year.

Introductory Exercises

A.   Match each word with its definition.

_____   1. growing higher; becoming more

_____   2. a company or person that
              makes products

_____   3. related to your job

_____   4. to give something that might
              be accepted

_____   5. to talk together in order to
              reach an understanding

_____   6. the workers

_____   7. to make something more difficult

_____   8. words about how something looks

_____   9. to fight with words

_____ 10. something you tried hard
              to do and finished

a. accomplishment
b. argue
c. complicate
d. description
e. increasing
f. manufacturer
g. negotiate
h. occupational
i. offer
j. staff
k. state
l. stress

B.   Answer **TRUE** or **FALSE**.

_____   1. People usually like to be under stress.

_____   2. A laborious job is one that requires a lot of work.

_____   3. A negotiator only listens; he never talks.

_____   4. A person must accept the first job offer he receives.

_____   5. Accomplishing something complicated is very satisfying.

_____   6. An executive makes many important business decisions.

_____   7. Meat, fruit, and vegetables are manufactured products.

_____   8. Prices will increase when there is less of a product available.

Study Exercises

C. Match each word with a related word. (The related word may be a synonym **or** a word that often occurs with the first one.) Use each word only once.

____	1. accomplish	**a.**	profession
____	2. executive	**b.**	accept
____	3. stress	**c.**	contract
____	4. state	**d.**	difficulty
____	5. offer	**e.**	products
____	6. occupation	**f.**	fight
____	7. negotiate	**g.**	condition
____	8. manufacture	**h.**	worry
____	9. complication	**i.**	manager
____	10. argue	**j.**	succeed

D. In the blanks, write the appropriate word(s) from the word form chart in this unit.

1. Teaching young children is a very demanding _____ .

2. The business is in such a terrible state that the boss is feeling a lot of _____ .

3. Beginning in an unimportant job and becoming president of the company in five years is a big _____ .

4. After long contract _____-s , the staff and executives could not come to a decision.

5. These products are not handmade; they were _____-ed by machine.

6. Our boss always wants everything _____ . He can never wait for anything and never gives us enough time.

7. We were afraid he would leave the company, so we _____-ed him an increase in salary and a new office.

8. The _____-s of the company met to make decisions concerning the staff, cost increases, and manufacturing methods.

9. Our company uses a very _____ method to manufacture these products; other companies use easier methods.

10. We had an _____ in business this month; we sold more products than we usually do.

E. Read the passage and answer the questions that follow.

One of my biggest wishes was to start a business on my own. I was tired of my occupation and wanted to change jobs, so a friend and I decided to open a restaurant. We made all kinds of plans but did not know how complicated everything
5 was going to be!
First, we had to negotiate with several banks to get a loan. The bank executive at National Bank decided that he could not give us any money no matter how much we argued that we could pay it back. We finally got enough money,
10 however, and then had to find a small building to buy or rent.
After we got the loans and the building, we hired a company to modernize the inside of the building. We described how we wanted the restaurant to look, and after all the contracts were signed, the men began the laborious job of
15 putting in new walls, floors, and windows. Before the men finished, however, the executives of the company wanted to increase the cost. My friend told him that we had already negotiated a contract. They could not argue. Their men completed the job as planned in the beginning.
20 After they finished the building, we had to buy furniture, plates, and other restaurant items. To save money, we bought our tables and chairs from the manufacturer instead of from a store. We also had to hire a staff of experienced waiters and waitresses and several expert cooks. Because we offered good
25 salaries, it was not difficult to find the kind of staff we wanted.
Before we opened the restaurant, we carefully described to the staff how the restaurant was going to work. Each member of the staff was going to have certain responsibilities.
30 I would be the executive responsible for business, that is, taking care of bank accounts, paying bills and salaries, etc. My friend would manage the preparation of food and the staff.
When the restaurant finally opened, business was slow,
35 and a lack of money put stress on both my friend and me. We put some advertisements in the newspapers and on the radio. These helped to increase our business, and now everything is fine; in fact, our restaurant has become one of the most popular in the city. My friend and I see this
40 restaurant as our biggest accomplishment.

1. Why did John want to start a business? _____

_____

2. He and his friend made careful plans, but what surprised them? ___

_____

3. What did they have to do first? _____

_____

4. Who would not give them money? _____

_____

5. What was the next thing they had to do? _____

_____

6. How did the men from the building company know where to put

the new walls and windows? _____

_____

7. What complication did John and his friend have with the building

company? _____

_____

8. What did John's friend tell the company executive? _____

_____

9. How did they save money on their restaurant furniture? _____

_____

10. Why was it easy to find a good staff? _____

_____

11. What were the work responsibilities of John and his friend? _____

_____

12. How did John and his friend feel when the restaurant opened?

Why? _____

_____

13. How did the advertisements help them? _____

_____

14. How do John and his friend now feel about the restaurant? _____

_____

Follow-up

F.   Dictation: Write the sentences that your teacher reads aloud.

1. _____

2. _____

3. _____

4. _____

5. _____

G.   Complete the sentence with a word from the word form chart in this unit.

1. The _____ really respects the boss.

2. Too much _____ on the job can sometimes make employees ill.

3. He is so lazy! He never wants to do the _____ jobs.

4. Mary didn't take a vacation when her boss _____ her time off.

5. Negotiating the important contract with the auto manufacturer was his biggest _____ this year.

6. I couldn't remember what the machine looked like, so he _____ it to me.

7. They don't think alike on any subject; therefore, they always have _____ .

8. The president of a company can also be called a(n)

   _____ .

9. Teaching is very difficult _____ .

10. The price of products is _____ because the cost of manufacturing has gotten higher.

H.   Answer the following questions.

1. What type of manufactured products does your city produce?
2. What state are you in after a difficult day at work?
3. Think of several different occupations. What is a good salary offer for each?

4. Describe the responsibilities of an executive.
5. What is your biggest accomplishment in the last five years? How did you accomplish this? Why was this important?
6. What is the most complicated decision you have made?
7. What kinds of complications can be caused by working, studying, and taking care of a family all at once?

Transportation

Word Form Chart

NOUN	VERB	ADJECTIVE	ADVERB	PREPOSITION
	back up			
		backward	backward(s)	
continuation	continue	continued		
		continuing		
		continuous	continuously	
		continual	continually	
exit	exit			
hole				
inspection	inspect	inspected		
journey	journey			
load	load	loaded		
		loading		
motor		motorized		
motorist				
passenger				
reason	reason	reasonable	reasonably	
signal	signal			
speed	speed (sped, sped)	speeding		
trucker				
vehicle		vehicular		
				via

Definitions and Examples

1. **speed** (a) [how fast something goes]

    Drivers should be careful of their **speed** in the cities.
    They drove their cars at a high **speed**.

    (b) [to go too fast]

    Speeding often leads to car accidents.

2. **motor** [an engine]

    Drivers sometimes have trouble with their car **motors** in hot
    weather.

3. **motorist** [an automobile driver]

    Motorists should drive carefully.

4. **vehicle** [a device with wheels used to carry people or things]

    Cars, buses, and trains are all **vehicles**.
    There were many **vehicles** on the road.

5. **truck** [a vehicle used to carry things]

    The **truck** carried the food from the farms to the stores.
    Special **trucks** are used to take new cars to where they will be sold.

6. **passenger** [a person who rides in a vehicle]

    He drove so fast that he frightened his **passengers**.
    Our car easily carries five **passengers**.

7. **load** [anything a vehicle or a person carries]

    The truck carried a heavy **load** of bricks.
    The truck lost its **load** in the middle of the highway.

8. **signal** [to give a sign that communicates a message]

    The motorist **signaled** that he was going to turn.
    The policeman **signaled** for us to pull to the side of the road.
    We didn't see the traffic **signal** and didn't stop for the red light.

9. **journey** [a long trip]

    They took a **journey** across the country.
    Their **journey** was long, hot, and tiring.

10. **exit** [the place where you leave a highway, parking lot, building, etc.]

   The truck got off the highway at **Exit** 14.
   The parking lot had only one **exit**.
   The **exit** and entrance to the highway are very near each other.

11. **back up** (separable) [to lead with the back first]

   The driver **backed** his car **up** without looking and hit the car
      behind him.
   Back up. You've gone too far.

12. **backward(s)** [with the back first or leading]

   The car went **backwards** and then forward again to get into the
      parking space.
   The numbers were written **backwards**, so we could not understand
      them.

13. **via** [by way of]

   We went **via** Philadelphia on our way to New York.
   They sent their furniture to their new town **via** truck.

14. **hole** [an opening, frequently unwanted]

   The **holes** in the road caused many problems for the motorists.
   The stone hit the car window and made a **hole** in it.

15. **continue** [to do something without stopping]

   They **continued** driving down the highway.
   The trucker **continued** to speed after he was arrested for speeding.
   After eating dinner, the motorists **continued** on their way.

16. **inspect** [to examine, usually to find problems]

   The car was **inspected** at the garage.
   The load was **inspected** before the truck could cross into the
      neighboring country.
   They found many holes in the car during the **inspection**.

17. **reason** (for) [an explanation; why]

   Sorry I'm late. The **reason** is that I was stopped for speeding.

   A: Why did the police stop John?
   B: I don't know. He didn't tell me the **reason**.

Introductory Exercises

A.   Match each word with its definition.

       ___ **1.** to examine carefully

       ___ **2.** a rider

       ___ **3.** how fast

       ___ **4.** by way of

       ___ **5.** a large vehicle

       ___ **6.** the way out

       ___ **7.** an engine

       ___ **8.** anything that is carried

       ___ **9.** an explanation

      ___ **10.** a long trip

a. exit
b. hole
c. inspect
d. journey
e. load
f. motor
g. passenger
h. reason
i. speed
j. truck
k. vehicle
l. via

B.   Complete the sentence with a word from the word form chart in this unit.

1. If you want to move furniture, you can use a(n) _____ .

2. If you are going to turn, you should put on your turn

     _____ .

3. If you are in the car and are not driving, then you are

     a(n) _____ .

4. The police might stop you if you _____ .

5. When I _____-ed my car, I found many problems.

6. Truckers frequently have to make long cross country

     _____ .

7. A truck carries its _____ in the back.

8. He wasn't tired, so he _____-ed driving to the next city.

Study Exercises

C. Circle the word or phrase which is different in meaning.

1. to exit   to leave   to get off   to arrive   to go out of

2. driver   motorist   trucker   vehicle   pilot

3. backward   to the left   exit   to the right   forward

4. journey   load   trip   vacation   travels

5. motor   train   truck   automobile   taxi

D. Write the word that best describes the examples listed.

directions
vehicles
speeds
signals
size
loads

1. _____ big, small, large

2. _____ green light, stop, red light

3. _____ passengers, food, products

4. _____ north, backward, left

5. _____ truck, car, bus

6. _____ 55 miles an hour, fast, slow

E. Read the passage and answer the questions that follow.

The highways in the United States are reasonably good, and it is not complicated to drive on them, but before a motorist begins driving long distances, he should learn some basics about the highways and about certain laws.

5   Highways in the United States are numbered to show the direction of the highway. Highways with a number ending in 0, 2, 4, 6, or 8—for example, Hwy* 30 or Hwy 72—go in an east-west direction. Highways numbered with 1, 3, 5, 7, or 9—for example, Hwy 79 or 95—go north and south. Three

10   numbers, such as 495 or 376, show that the highway circles a city so that motorists can avoid the downtown area or heavy city traffic.

Most highway exits are very clear, with the exit name and number on a sign above the road. Exits may lead to a

15   town or onto another highway. On some highways, the exit lane is also the entrance lane for cars coming onto the highways (see picture on next page). For this reason, motorists must be careful to use turn signals when exiting so that they don't cause an accident with entering vehicles.

---

*Hwy—the abbreviation for highway

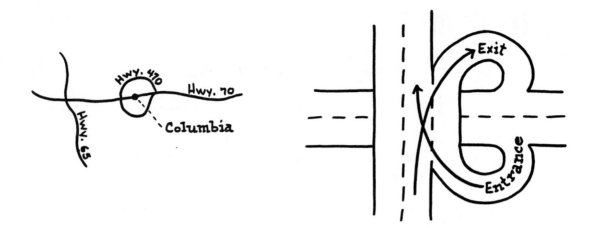

20   The speed limit on many large highways is 65 miles, or about 106 kilometers, an hour. The speed is always lower on exits and entrances and is frequently lower when a highway passes through a heavily populated area. It is the law that motorists stay at or below the speed limit and pay attention
25 to all traffic signals. It is also the law in many parts of the country that motorists wear safety belts.** This is true for the passengers as well as for the driver of the vehicle. Motorists must also never throw anything out of the car windows. There are many laws against leaving paper and
30 garbage on the highways.

       If motorists remember how highways are numbered, drive within the speed limit, and pay attention to other rules of the road, they should have no problems driving on U.S. highways.

1. How do motorists know which direction they are traveling? _____

_____

2. Why do some roads have three numbers? _____

_____

3. How do motorists know which exit is next? _____

_____

4. What is unusual about highway exits in some parts of the United

States? _____

_____

**A safety belt or seat belt is the device on each car seat that helps the passenger stay safely in his seat during an accident.

5. What must motorists be sure to do when exiting (or changing lanes)?

_____

_____

6. What is the speed limit on most highways in the United States?

When is it different? _____

_____

7. What are several laws that motorists should remember? _____

_____

F.   Write the correct words in the blanks.

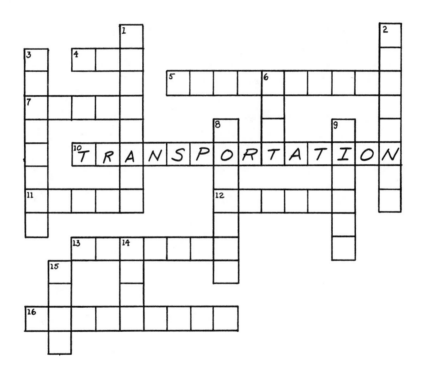

ACROSS	DOWN
4. on; through; by way of	**1.** the opposite of forward
5. an examination of a vehicle	**2.** to go without stopping
7. a motorized vehicle	**3.** a driver
10. moving something from one place to another	**6.** where you go out
11. how fast	**8.** a trip
12. an explanation	**9.** a device or movement used to communicate
13. a device with wheels used to carry things	**14.** a bad part in the road that drivers avoid hitting
16. riders	**15.** anything a vehicle or a person carriers

Follow-up

G. Dictation: Write the sentences that your teacher reads aloud.

1. _____

2. _____

3. _____

4. _____

5. _____

H. Answer the following questions.

1. What reasons would a motorist have for driving backwards?
2. What are some typical loads that trucks carry?
3. What are some typical signals used to control traffic?
4. What traffic laws must motorists pay attention to in your country?
5. What are some problems large trucks can cause for car drivers?
6. Where is vehicular or motorized traffic usually not permitted? Why?
7. Which traffic signals do you think are the most important ones?
8. Describe the longest journey you have ever made.
9. How old must a person be to drive a motorized vehicle in your country?

Clothing

Word Form Chart

NOUN	VERB	ADJECTIVE	ADVERB
alteration	alter	altered	
		unaltered	
appearance	appear		
custom		customary	customarily
		fancy	
fashion		fashionable	fashionably
		unfashionable	unfashionably
fit	fit	fitted	
fur		furry	
genuineness		genuine	genuinely
	loosen	loose	loosely
nakedness		naked	
popularity	popularize	popular	popularly
		unpopular	
		practical	practically
		impractical	
removal	remove	removable	
spot		spotted	
	suit	suitable	suitably
		unsuitable	unsuitably

Definitions and Examples

1. **custom** [the usual way of doing something]

   It is the **custom** in some countries to take off your shoes before entering someone's home.

   A: Is it **customary** for men to kiss each other when they meet in your country?
   B: No. We do not have that **custom** in our country.

2. **alter** [to change something; to make something be different]

   I had to **alter** all of my clothes because I lost weight last year.

   A: Can you help me **alter** my dress for the party?
   B: Yes. I'll help you with the **alterations**.

3. **appear** [to seem; to look like]

   She **appears** to be a rich person because she buys expensive clothes.

   A: Did you see Joan at the party last night?
   B: Yes, I did. She **appeared** to be very happy with her new boyfriend.

4. **fancy** [very good or expensive]

   Helen buys **fancy** dresses because she goes to many formal parties.

   A: Did you see Pat's **fancy** new sportscar?
   B: Yes. It was a gift from his rich uncle.

5. **fashion** [the way many people like to dress at a certain time]

   Long dresses and skirts were in **fashion** last year.
   Long coats were **fashionable** too.

   A: What kind of clothes does Mary like to buy?
   B: Mary only buys clothes that are in **fashion**.

6. **fit** [to be the correct size]

   This dress doesn't **fit** well. It's too large.

   A: Your jacket won't **fit** my sister.
   B: Why not?
   A: Because my sister is smaller than you.

7. **fur** [the soft, thick hair of some animals]

   Fur coats and jackets are very fashionable in many Western countries.

   A: My mother wants to buy a **fur** hat.
   B: Why?
   A: Because **fur** hats are in fashion now.

8. **remove** [to take off or away]

  It is customary in some countries for men to **remove** their hats when they enter a house or a public building.

  Patient: I think I broke my arm.
  Doctor: Let's **remove** your jacket, and I will examine your arm.

9. **genuine** [not false]

  That fur coat is **genuine**. It is not man-made.

  A: How do you know her fur coat is **genuine**?
  B: Because she bought it in an expensive fur shop.

10. **loose** [not tight]

  This jacket fits too **loosely**. I should alter it.

  A: Did you lose weight?
  B: Yes, and now all of my clothes are too **loose**.

11. **naked** [not wearing clothes]

  The children swam **naked** in the ocean.
  It is sometimes necessary to be almost **naked** for a medical examination.

12. **popular** [liked by many people]

  That type of skirt is very **popular** this year.

  A: What type of women's clothing is **popular** now in your country?
  B: Long skirts and short jackets are **popular** now.

13. **practical** [good for wear or use]

  This dress is very **practical** because I can wear it to work or to parties.

  A: Are those shoes **practical** for taking long walks?
  B: Yes. They are very comfortable.

14. **spot** [a dark color on clothing made by food, grass, coffee, etc.]

  She used water to remove the **spot** on his shirt.
  Her dress was old and covered with **spots**.

  A: How did you get those green **spots** on your shirt?
  B: I fell on the grass during a football game.

15. **suitable** [correct for what is needed; appropriate]

  Those clothes are **suitable** for a wedding.

  A: Is this cotton dress **suitable** for the party?
  B: No. It's not **suitable**. You should wear a formal dress to the party.

Introductory Exercises

A. Match each word with its definition.

_____	1. to be the correct size	**a.** alter
_____	2. not false	**b.** custom
_____	3. liked by many people	**c.** fancy
_____	4. to take off or away	**d.** fashion
_____	5. correct for what is needed	**e.** fit
_____	6. not tight	**f.** fur
_____	7. to change something	**g.** genuine
_____	8. the way many people like to	**h.** loose
	dress at a certain time	**i.** naked
_____	9. the thick, soft hair of some animals	**j.** popular
_____	10. not wearing clothes	**k.** remove
		l. suitable

B. Answer each question with a word from the word chart in this unit.

1. What is a material that jackets and coats are made of?
2. What kind of clothes do you wear to a formal party?
3. How do clothes fit after you lose weight?
4. How do you describe someone who is not wearing clothes?
5. What kinds of clothes and music do young people like?
6. How do you describe clothes that many people are wearing at a certain time?
7. What should a man do with his hat when he enters a room?
8. What must you do to your clothes if they do not fit correctly?
9. What kind of shoes should you wear for long walks in the country?

Study Exercises

C. Choose one of the following prefixes to form the negative meaning of these words from the word form chart.

	un-	im-
1. fashionable	_____	fashionable
2. practical	_____	practical
3. popular	_____	popular
4. suitable	_____	suitable
5. altered	_____	altered

Match the words that have similar meanings.

_____ **1.** alter   **a.** way
                                       b. clothes
_____ **2.** fashions   **c.** hair
_____ **3.** suitable   **d.** change
_____ **4.** fur   **e.** appropriate
_____ **5.** custom

D. Write **T** if the answer is true and **F** if it is false.

_____ **1.** If a jacket fits, you should alter it.
_____ **2.** You can eat fancy food in an expensive restaurant.
_____ **3.** Some people will only wear clothes that are in fashion.
_____ **4.** Fur coats are expensive.
_____ **5.** All shoes are made of genuine leather.
_____ **6.** Loose fitting clothes are comfortable.
_____ **7.** It is difficult to remove some spots from clothing.
_____ **8.** Fancy clothes are suitable for formal parties.
_____ **9.** It is customary to swim naked in most countries.
_____ **10.** Many young people like to buy popular fashions.

E. In the blanks, write the appropriate word(s) from the word form chart in this unit.

1. After I lost weight, my belt wasn't tight. It was _____ .
2. He has the _____ of a rich man because he always wears fancy clothes.
3. His boots are made of _____ leather.
4. This jacket doesn't _____ well. It's too small.
5. Rich people like to buy _____ clothes and cars.
6. Short, cotton skirts are in _____ this summer.
7. Many young people enjoy wearing fashions that are

_____ .

8. A cup of coffee fell on my skirt. Now I have brown

_____ -s all over it.

9. I asked the man in front of me to _____ his hat because I couldn't see the teacher.
10. When clothes do not fit well, they should be _____ -ed .
11. Children should wear _____ clothes that are strong and comfortable.

F. Circle the word which is different in meaning.

1. suitable   fancy   correct
2. practical   comfortable   bargain
3. genuine   alter   change
4. fashionable   practical   popular
5. hair   fur   spot
6. customary   naked   uncovered

G. Read the dialogue and answer the questions that follow.

Cathy: My boyfriend took me to a fancy party last night.
Amy: What did you wear?
Cathy: I wore my blue dress. It was the only suitable dress I had.
5   Amy: But you've lost weight. Isn't that dress a little loose?
Cathy: No. It fits perfectly. I didn't have to make any alterations.
Amy: That's great! Now tell me about the party. Did you see any famous people?
10   Cathy: Well, the party was held at a fashionable restaurant. There were a lot of young, popular singers there, and everyone was wearing the latest fashions. One woman wore a beautiful long fur coat. Another one wore a dress of genuine leather!
15   Amy: Did you have a good time?
Cathy: Yes. We were having a good time, but then something terrible happened.
Amy: What happened?
Cathy: A piece of cake fell on my dress and made a big
20   spot! I wanted to leave the party, but I was able to remove the spot with soap and water. I was so glad.

1. Where did Cathy go last night? _____

_____

2. Why did she wear her blue dress? _____

_____

3. How did the dress fit? _____

_____

4. Did she have to make any alterations? _____

_____

5. Where was the party held? _____

_____

6. What kind of people were at the party? _____

_____

7. Describe the clothes that the women wore. _____

_____

8. What terrible thing happened to Cathy? _____

_____

9. What did Cathy do to the spot? _____

_____

Follow-up

H. Dictation: Write the sentences that your teacher reads aloud.

1. _____

2. _____

3. _____

4. _____

5. _____

I.   Answer the following questions.

1. What fashions are most popular in your country today?
2. Who alters your clothes if they do not fit you?
3. Do you prefer to wear practical shoes or fashionable shoes? Why?
4. What clothing customs do people follow in your country?
5. What kinds of clothes are suitable for school in your country?
6. Do you prefer tight or loose fitting clothes?
7. Are fur coats and jackets fashionable in your country?
8. What colors of clothes are most popular in your country?
9. What do you do when a friend of yours appears sad?

J. Talk about one of the following subjects:

    a. Fashions in your country
    b. Customs in your country
    c. Ways to remove spots on your clothes

Communication

Word Form Chart

NOUN	VERB	ADJECTIVE	ADVERB
abbreviation	abbreviate	abbreviated	
abruptness		abrupt	abruptly
code	code	coded	
contact	contact		
copy	copy	copied	
		direct	directly
existence	exist	existing	
familiarity	familiarize	familiar	familiarly
mile			
promptness		prompt	promptly
rapidity		rapid	rapidly
regularity	regularize	regular	regularly
irregularity		irregular	irregularly
route	route		
second			
sidewalk			
sticker	stick (stuck, stuck)	sticky	
stickiness			
		stuck	
telegram			
wrap	wrap	wrapped	
		wrapping	

Definitions and Examples

1. **abbreviate** [to make something shorter]

    The **abbreviation** of "United States" is "U.S."
    The **abbreviated** interview lasted only fifteen minutes.

2. **abrupt** [not expected]

    The taxi made an **abrupt** stop at the intersection.
    The angry husband turned **abruptly** and left the room.

3. **code** [letters, numbers or symbols that have a special meaning]

    The ZIP **code** in an address shows a person's neighborhood.
    The area **code** is part of your telephone number.

4. **contact** (a) [to communicate with]

    Contact your landlord about the broken window.
    Do not lose **contact** with your family.

    (b) [to come together]

    Do not let water come in **contact** with that special clothing.

5. **copy** [something that is made to look like something else]

    The secretary made a **copy** of my letter.
    You should not **copy** your friends' homework.

6. **route** [the way]

    What is the best **route** to the library?
    That **route** is dangerous for a car in winter.

7. **direct** [in the shortest way]

    I always take the most **direct** route to school.
    We went **directly** to the movie. We didn't stop at the restaurant
    first.

8. **exist** [to be; to live]

    Most animals cannot **exist** without water.
    Many problems **exist** in poor countries.
    I cannot prove the **existence** of the ice age.

9. **familiar** (with) [knowing something well]

    I am **familiar with** New York. I was born there.
    I am not **familiar with** that author. I have never read her books.

10. **mile** [a distance of 5,280 feet; about 1.6 kilometers]

> I walk two **miles** to school.
> A long distance runner can run for many **miles**.

11. **prompt** [on time; not late]

> Please be **prompt** for the interview. An employer doesn't like to wait.
> If you don't arrive **promptly**, you will miss the bus.

12. **rapid** [fast]

> An airplane is **rapid** transportation.
> Some secretaries can type **rapidly**.

13. **regular** [usual]

> **Regular** body temperature is 98.6 degrees Fahrenheit.
> My schedule is **irregular** today because it's a holiday.

14. **second** [1/60 of a minute]

> One **second** passes very fast.
> There are 60 **seconds** in one minute.
> He won the race by several **seconds**.

15. **sidewalk** [the place for walking by the side of the street]

> There are no **sidewalks** in rural areas.
> City **sidewalks** are often crowded.

16. **stick** [to put something in a place and make it stay there]

> A stamp will **stick** to an envelope.
> **Stick** the sign on the wall so that everyone can see it.
> Cut grass **sticks** to my shoes.

17. **telegram** [a message sent in code by electricity]

> We received many **telegrams** on our wedding day.
> A long **telegram** can be expensive.

18. **wrap** [to put a cover around something]

> The gifts were **wrapped** in pretty paper.
> You should **wrap** the package before you go to the post office.

Introductory Exercises

A. Match each word with its definition.

_____ 1. not expected

_____ 2. to live

_____ 3. knowing something well

_____ 4. the way

_____ 5. 5,280 feet

_____ 6. usual

_____ 7. 1/60 of a minute

_____ 8. to make shorter

a. abbreviate
b. abrupt
c. code
d. exist
e. familiar with
f. mile
g. regular
h. route
i. second
j. wrap

B. Answer each question with a word from the word chart in this unit.

1. What do you call 5,280 feet?
2. Describe a person who is always on time.
3. How does an airplane travel?
4. Where should you walk?
5. How can you send a long distance message?
6. What must you do to a package before you mail it?
7. What route should you take home? (3 answers)

Study Exercises

C. Circle the word which is different in meaning.

1. live   exist   die
2. way   coast   route
3. wrap   gloves   cover
4. army   short   abbreviated
5. regular   enough   usual
6. supply   meet   contact
7. fast   damage   rapid

D. In the blanks, write the appropriate word(s) from the word form chart in this unit.

1. If you don't understand the contract, you should _____ your lawyer.
2. I'll show you the best _____ if you give me that map.
3. The weather changed _____ , and I didn't have my raincoat.
4. It takes only a few _____ -s to dial the telephone.
5. Some automobile races are hundreds of _____ -s long.
6. If you like this photograph, I'll have a(n) _____ made for you.
7. You must put water on a stamp to make it _____ .

E. Write **T** if the sentence is true and **F** if it is false.

____ 1. A second is a very long time.
____ 2. Addresses in the United States should have a ZIP code.
____ 3. The abbreviation for "street" is "St."
____ 4. A mailman is familiar with his regular route.
____ 5. The direct route is the longest route.
____ 6. Problems exist in every neighborhood.
____ 7. Houses are built on the sidewalk.
____ 8. Rice sometimes sticks to the pot.

F. Read the passage and answer the questions that follow.

      Telephones in the United States are usually rapid and inexpensive. Telephones can be found in public places and in almost every home and business in the country. It would be difficult for most Americans to think of existing without
5   them.
      If you need to contact someone many miles away, you need to know his area code and phone number. It takes only a few seconds for a regular call to be completed.
      You can also send a telegram using your telephone. The
10 message is sent promptly, and a printed copy can also be delivered. Many people prefer telephone communication over mail communication. With a telephone there are no packages to wrap and no stamps to stick on envelopes.

Write **T** if the sentence is true and **F** if it is false.

_____ **1.** Telephones usually cost a lot of money.

_____ **2.** Most people in the United States have a telephone.

_____ **3.** An area code is necessary for a long distance call.

_____ **4.** Calls can be completed in a short time.

_____ **5.** You cannot use your phone to send a telegram.

_____ **6.** A telegram message is sent promptly.

_____ **7.** Many people like telephone more than mail.

Follow-up

G. Dictation: Write the sentences that your teacher reads aloud.

1. _____

2. _____

3. _____

4. _____

5. _____

H. Answer the following questions.

1. Have you ever sent or received a telegram? Describe what you did.
2. How much does it cost to operate a copy machine?
3. How many languages are you familiar with?
4. Are there sidewalks in your city?
5. Is the mail rapid in your country?
6. Are the buses prompt in your country?
7. Do you come to school by the same route every day?
8. How many miles do you walk or drive to school every day?
9. Does your country use ZIP codes? What is your ZIP code?

I. Describe the most direct route to 1. the library
                                         2. the bookstore
                                         3. your apartment

Environment

Word Form Chart

NOUN	VERB	ADJECTIVE	ADVERB	PREPOSITION
			below	below
bottom		bottom		
device	devise			
drill	drill	drilling		
		drilled		
estimate	estimate	estimated		
expansion	expand	expanding		
		expanded		
			forever	
layer	layer	layered		
object				
permanence		permanent	permanently	
process	process	processed		
reality		real	really	
		unreal		
separation	separate	separate	separately	
simplicity	simplify	simple	simply	
solution	solve			
substance		substantial	substantially	
surface	surface			
volume		voluminous		
			within	within

Definitions and Examples

1. **below** [lower than; under]

    During our airplane trip we saw the sky above and the land **below**.

    A: Are all rivers above the ground?
    B: No. Some rivers are **below** ground.

2. **bottom** [the lowest part of something]

    The rock fell to the **bottom** of the pond.

    A: Why is it so difficult to explore the **bottom** of the ocean?
    B: Because some parts are very deep.

3. **devise** [to plan; to invent]

    They **devised** a better method for oil production.

    A: Can they **devise** a plan to stop air pollution in the city?
    B: They **devised** a plan last year, but it wasn't successful.

4. **simple** [easy; not difficult]

    The answer to the problem is **simple**.

    A: Can you devise a **simple** method to prevent water pollution?
    B: No. It's not a **simple** problem.

5. **estimate** [to guess the size, weight, or cost of something]

    He **estimated** the length of the house to be 40 feet.

    A: How much do you think that chair weighs?
    B: I **estimate** that it weighs five pounds.

6. **expand** (a) [to get larger]

    Wooden doors **expand** in hot, wet weather.

    A: Why are the roads in such bad condition?
    B: **Expansion** in hot weather causes damage to the roads.

    (b) [to make larger]

    We **expanded** our house when we had a second baby.

7. **forever** [always; without end]

    Nothing lasts **forever**. Everything changes.

    A: Why doesn't someone invent a car that will last **forever**?
    B: Because the automobile factories wouldn't make any money!

8. **layer** [one thickness; things that are placed over the top of another thing]

    The engineers told us to put **layers** of sand bags along the river to prevent flooding.

    A: Did you see Jim's house after the flood?
    B: Yes. There were **layers** of mud and dirt all over the floors and furniture.

9. **object** [a thing that you can see or feel]

    There was a strange wooden **object** in the package.

    A: What **objects** does Marge want to sell?
    B: She wants to sell her table and chairs, and some plates and glasses, too.

10. **permanent** [not changing; staying forever]

    The coffee made a **permanent** spot on her dress.

    A: Can pollution cause **permanent** damage?
    B: Yes. Pollution caused by industrial chemicals can injure a person's health **permanently**.

11. **process** [a way of doing or making something]

    The **process** of making a cake is easy.

    A: Do you know how oil is **processed** to make gasoline?
    B: I'm not sure about the **process**, but I do know that it's expensive.

12. **drill** [to make holes with a machine that moves in a circle]

    Drilling for oil can pollute the environment.

    A: Where does the oil company plan to **drill** for oil?
    B: In the ocean.

13. **real** [correct; genuine; true]

    The ring was made out of **real** gold.

    A: Why was your sister so frightened?
    B: Terrible storms **really** frighten her.

14. **separate** [divided; not together]

    The corn and the wheat are processed in **separate** buildings.

    A: Did you know that someone invented a process to **separate** the salt from the water in the ocean?
    B: Really? That's great!

15. **solution** [the answer to a question or problem]

    They found a simple **solution** to the problem.

    A: How can we **solve** the problem of not enough fuel?
    B: Using the power of the sun is one of the best **solutions**.

16. **substance** [a solid or liquid; a material]

    Water, milk, and wood are **substances**.

    A: There is a dark, oily **substance** in the river water.
    B: Yes. I know. It came from a chemical leak at a factory two miles from here.

17. **surface** [the outer or upper part of something]

    Men have landed on the **surface** of the moon.
    He swam below the **surface** of the lake.

    A: Did you know there was a major accident off the east coast today?
    B: Yes. Oil leaked from a big ship and is floating on the **surface** of the water.

18. **volume** (a) [the amount of space an object takes; the amount of liquid something can hold]

    A: How do you find the **volume** of a box?
    B: You multiply the height by the width by the length of the box to find the **volume**.

    (b) [how loud something is]

    The TV is too loud. Turn down the **volume**.

19. **within** [inside]

    He was **within** five miles of his home when the accident occurred.

    A: Don't put those chemicals **within** eight feet of the water!
    B: Right. We have to be careful.

Introductory Exercises

A.   Match each word with its definition.

____	**1.** to plan	**a.**	below
____	**2.** genuine	**b.**	bottom
____	**3.** to get larger	**c.**	devise
____	**4.** the lowest part	**d.**	drill
____	**5.** unchanging	**e.**	estimate
____	**6.** to make holes	**f.**	expand
____	**7.** an answer	**g.**	object
____	**8.** to guess	**h.**	permanent
____	**9.** a thing	**i.**	real
____	**10.** inside	**j.**	simple
____	**11.** the space something takes	**k.**	solution
____	**12.** the top	**l.**	substance
____	**13.** easy	**m.**	surface
		n.	volume
		o.	within

B.   Answer **TRUE** or **FALSE**.

1. A cake can have several layers.
2. Death is permanent.
3. A dream is real.
4. Married people never separate.
5. International law is simple.
6. A storm lasts forever.
7. A drill is a tool.
8. Tennis is a process.
9. Gold is a substance.
10. The earth is below the sky.
11. Clouds are at the bottom of the ocean.
12. Estimates are usually exact.
13. You can float on the surface of a lake.

Study Exercises

C. Match the words that have opposite meanings.

　　　____ 1. bottom
　　　____ 2. below
　　　____ 3. separate
　　　____ 4. simple
　　　____ 5. solution
　　　____ 6. permanent

　　　a. changing
　　　b. together
　　　c. difficult
　　　d. top
　　　e. problem
　　　f. above

Match the words that have similar meanings.

　　　____ 1. estimate
　　　____ 2. forever
　　　____ 3. object
　　　____ 4. real
　　　____ 5. separate
　　　____ 6. solution

　　　a. different
　　　b. genuine
　　　c. answer
　　　d. thing
　　　e. guess
　　　f. always

D. Write **T** if the sentence is true and **F** if it is false.

　　　____ 1. Oil floats on the bottom of a lake.
　　　____ 2. When a substance expands, it gets bigger.
　　　____ 3. There are many layers of rock underground.
　　　____ 4. Chemicals cannot cause permanent damage to the environment.
　　　____ 5. Part of the process of making dinner is cleaning up.
　　　____ 6. There is a simple solution to the problem of air pollution in major cities.
　　　____ 7. You can live on this earth forever.
　　　____ 8. You can drill holes in a liquid substance.

E. In the blanks, write the appropriate word(s) from the word form chart in this unit.

　　1. You can _____ your knowledge of the environment by reading about it.
　　2. Machines cannot last _____ . They always require repairs.

3. Someone should _____ a better method to

_____ for oil.

4. There is _____ danger that industrial chemicals

will damage people's health _____ .

5. Many ships damaged in terrible storms are at the _____

of the ocean.

6. Fish swim _____ the _____ of the water.

7. In mathematics class I had to find the _____ of a

large box.

8. They can only _____ the amount of damage made by

the oil leak. They're still not certain of the exact amount.

9. If you put water and oil into a glass, they will _____

into two _____ -s .

10. A dark chemical _____ polluted the water.

F.   Circle the word which is different in meaning.

1. solution   answer   problem

2. drill   object   thing

3. permanently   forever   change

4. expand   space   volume

5. real   layer   genuine

6. devise   plan   problem

7. substance   surface   top

G.   Read the following passage and answer the questions that follow.

The discovery of gold on the west coast of the United
States in 1849 caused many people to move to California
permanently, hoping to become rich.

Gold is found in many places but in small supply. It is
5   often found on the surface of the earth. Since gold is a heavy
substance, it is sometimes found loose on the bottom of
rivers. The gold is found together with sand or rocks and
must be separated from them. It is simple to search for this
type of gold.

10   It is not usually necessary to drill for gold, but when a
layer of gold is located deep below the surface of the earth, it
is possible to drill a hole into the ground. Engineers have
developed modern processes for removing gold from rock.

Gold is not very hard, so it is sometimes melted and
15   added to other substances for making rings, coins, and art
objects. It will be prized forever because it is beautiful, rare,
and useful.

Write **T** if the sentence is true and **F** if it is false.

_____ **1.** Gold is so light that it floats in rivers.

_____ **2.** Many people moved to California to find gold.

_____ **3.** Gold cannot be separated from rock.

_____ **4.** Gold is sometimes found underground.

_____ **5.** Gold is very hard.

_____ **6.** Gold is beautiful, but not useful.

Follow-up

H. Dictation: Read the sentences that your teacher reads aloud.

1. _____

2. _____

3. _____

4. _____

5. _____

I. Answer the following questions.

1. Do you have air or water pollution in your country? Where?
2. Does your country have laws about pollution? Describe the laws.
3. Do storms cause much damage in your country? What kind of damage?
4. Can you estimate the number of people in your country?
5. Do families often live separately? Why?
6. Do most people have permanent employment? What types of employment are not permanent?
7. Has your country ever expanded? When?
8. Name a food in your country which has layers.
9. Do you expect to live in the same place forever?
10. What problem would you like your government to solve?

J. Tell a story:

1. Describe the process of cooking rice.
2. Describe the process of changing a wheel on a bicycle or car.

Media

Word Form Chart

NOUN	VERB	ADJECTIVE	ADVERB	PREPO-SITION	CON-JUNC-TION
attitude					
basis	base	basic	basically		
base		based			
biography		biographical			
category	categorize				
characteristic	characterize	characteristic	characteristically		
conclusion	conclude	conclusive	conclusively		
	convince	convincing	convincingly		
		convinced			
detail		detailed			
emphasis	emphasize	emphasized			
		emphatic	emphatically		
fiction		fictional			
nonfiction		nonfictional			
	follow	following			
negation	negate	negative			
					neither ...nor
phrase					
plural		plural			
		positive	positively		
recognition	recognize	recognizable			
revelation	reveal	revealing			
				through	

49

Definitions and Examples

1. **biography** [a book about a person's life]

   I am reading an interesting book, a **biography** of John Kennedy.
   The **biography** covers his life from his childhood until his death.

2. **reveal** [to show; to uncover something that was not obvious]

   That article **reveals** a lot of information about that politician.
   Some women do not want to **reveal** their true ages.

3. **attitude** [an opinion]

   The author revealed his **attitude** at the beginning of the book; he
      hates his subject.

   A: What is your **attitude** on the government's decision?
   B: I'm happy about it.

4. **positive** [liking something; having a good opinion]

   That article is very **positive**; everything it says is good.
   Employers want workers with **positive** attitudes.

5. **negative** [not liking something; having a bad opinion]

   Public opinion about building that new road is **negative**; people do
      not want to spend the money.
   I asked about handing my paper in late, but the professor's attitude
      was **negative**.

6. **characteristic** [something that is typical]

   His best **characteristic** is a positive attitude.

   A: What is **characteristic** of her books?
   B: Most of them have sad endings.

7. **phrase** [a group of words shorter than a sentence]

   That poem has many beautiful **phrases** in it.
   "Thank you" is a very important **phrase**.

8. **plural** [a word showing more than one]

   The words "media" and "books" are **plurals**.
   Most **plurals** in English end in "-s."

9. **conclusion** [an end; a result]

    The **conclusion** of the article was negative; the author does not believe that there is any hope.

    A: Is the **conclusion** of this book exciting?
    B: Yes. I couldn't stop reading until I finished it.

10. **basis** [the idea from which something starts; the part on which something rests]

    The **basis** for that movie is a famous book.
    The book is **based on** the author's experiences in the army.

11. **fiction** [a book or story that is not true]

    Is that book **fiction**, or is it based on something that really happened?
    Books that are historical **fiction** are based on something that really happened but are not totally true.

    A: Do you like to read **fiction**?
    B: No. I prefer biographies and historical novels.

12. **category** [a type; a kind]

    Each book in this library is with the other books of the same **category**; all the biographies are together and all the fiction books are together.

    A: Which age **category** are you in—20–29 or 30–39?
    B: The first one; I'm only 23!

13. **detail** [something small and frequently not important]

    When I read I can never remember the **details**.
    We failed the test because many of the questions were about **details**.

14. **emphasize** [to make very clear and important]

    That news article **emphasizes** only the negative things about our city.
    The end of the speech **emphasized** the president's opinion.

15. **neither . . . nor** [not . . . and not]

    Neither the book **nor** the movie was very good.
    His attitude is **neither** very positive **nor** very negative.

16. **convince** [to make someone believe something]

    My wife **convinced** me to be more careful about spending money.
    The argument in the book is very **convincing**; everyone who reads it believes it.

17. follow [to come after]

The movie **followed** the book by two years.
The conclusion of the speech **followed** several strong arguments.

18. recognize [to see something and understand it or remember it]

It is easy to **recognize** the author's attitude. It is clear from the first page that he loves his subject.

A: Do you **recognize** that actor?
B: I don't remember his name, but I've seen a couple of his movies.

19. through (a) [because of]

It is easy to understand his ideas **through** his books.

(b) [from one side to the other]

Glass is used to make windows because you can see **through** it.
We traveled **through** Germany on our way to Poland.

Introductory Exercises

A. Match each word with its definition.

_____ **1.** something that is typical
_____ **2.** to show
_____ **3.** to come after
_____ **4.** something small and frequently not important
_____ **5.** a book about a person's life
_____ **6.** not liking something
_____ **7.** an opinion
_____ **8.** to make very clear and important
_____ **9.** to make someone believe something
_____ **10.** liking something
_____ **11.** to see something and understand it
_____ **12.** a book or story that is not true
_____ **13.** an end, a result
_____ **14.** a group of words

a. attitude
b. base
c. biography
d. category
e. characteristic
f. conclusion
g. convince
h. detail
i. emphasize
j. fiction
k. follow
l. negative
m. neither . . . nor
n. phrase
o. plural
p. positive
q. recognize
r. reveal
s. through

B.   Complete each sentence with a word from the word form chart in this
unit.

   1. She's reading a _____ of Gandhi's life.
   2. I _____-ed an old friend in the crowd.
   3. His _____ about the military is very negative; he
      hates it.
   4. I like _____ books, not true ones.
   5. The beginning of the book was interesting, but I didn't like the
      _____ because it was too sad.
   6. That biography describes not only the important things in her life
      but also many small _____ .
   7. Fiction and nonfiction are two large _____ of books.
   8. The words "in the room" are a(n) _____ , not a
      sentence.
   9. World War II _____-ed World War I.
   10. Her book places a lot of importance on having money, but many
      people do not agree with this _____ .
   11. She looked _____ the curtain to see who was coming.

Study Exercises

C.   Write **T** if the sentence is true and **F** if it is false.

   ____ 1. People usually can recognize their friends.
   ____ 2. A fictional book tells a true story.
   ____ 3. People like it when the newspaper reveals private things about
         their family.
   ____ 4. "Media" is a plural word.
   ____ 5. When your attitude about something is positive, you do not
         like it.
   ____ 6. A biography can be fictional.
   ____ 7. The police often try to follow criminals.
   ____ 8. You can look through a solid wall.
   ____ 9. Neither grass nor the sky is green.

D. Match each word with its opposite.

____ **1.** conclusion	**a.** cover
____ **2.** fictional	**b.** biography
____ **3.** plural	**c.** come before
____ **4.** reveal	**d.** true
____ **5.** recognize	**e.** not know
____ **6.** emphasize	**f.** positive
____ **7.** negative	**g.** beginning
____ **8.** follow	**h.** phrase
	i. one
	j. show to be not important

E. Read the passage and answer the questions that follow.

A friend of mine is a writer who does book reviews for the town newspaper. I thought that this must be a very interesting job, and I asked him if he enjoyed his work. He replied that most of the time it was fun, but sometimes it
5 was really work.

The worst part is that he has to finish reading each book, even when he does not like it. For example, in some poorly written murder mysteries, the conclusion is revealed too early in the book, and it is boring to read to the end after
10 recognizing who has committed the murder. He also does not like reading non-fiction books in which the author's attitude is very strongly negative or positive. He feels that a book is not convincing if it only reveals one side of the story.

His favorite categories of books are biographies and
15 historical fiction. He especially likes these types of books because he learns many things through reading them.

1. What job does the friend have? _____

_____

2. Why does he not like some murder mysteries? _____

_____

3. What kind of non-fiction books does he not like? _____

Why? _____

4. What types of books does he like best? _____

Why? _____

Follow-up

F.   Dictation: Write the sentences that your teacher reads aloud.

1. _____

2. _____

3. _____

4. _____

5. _____

G.   Answer the following questions.

1. Who is your favorite author? Give some characteristics of his/her writing.
2. Do you like to read fiction or non-fiction? Why?
3. What biographies have you read? Did you like them?
4. In what types of classes do you have trouble remembering details?
5. Do you read book reviews in magazines and newspapers?
6. Does your language have plural and non-plural words? What is the difference between plural and non-plural when you say the words?
7. When you are speaking and you want to emphasize something, what do you do to give it emphasis?
8. What do you feel negative about? Why?
9. Describe something positive and something negative about the United States.

H.   Describe your favorite book. Why do you like it?

Vacation

Word Form Chart

NOUN	VERB	ADJECTIVE	ADVERB	PREPOSITION	CONJUNCTION
		accustomed to			
	afford	affordable	affordably		
altitude					
		casual	casually		
	deserve	deserving	deservedly		
end	end	endless	endlessly		
envy	envy	envious	enviously		
equal	equal	equal	equally		
equality					
expedition					
extra		extra			
intention	intend	intended			
		intending			
		intentional	intentionally		
procedure	proceed				
sunrise	rise (rose, risen)	rising			
rush	rush	rushing			
sight	sight				
sunset	set				
				toward	
view	view				
					whenever

Definitions and Examples

1. **accustomed to** [used to]

   My father is **accustomed to** reading the newspaper every day after dinner.

   A: Does George travel a lot?
   B: Yes. He's **accustomed to** traveling to Europe twice a year to visit his family.

2. **afford** [to be able to pay for]

   I cannot **afford** to take a long vacation this year.

   A: Ann isn't going to the beach this summer.
   B: Why not?
   A: She can't **afford** to pay for the hotel.

3. **altitude** [a height]

   The airplane was flying at an **altitude** of 20,000 feet.

   A: I don't like to climb high mountains.
   B: Why not?
   A: Because the air becomes thinner at high **altitudes**.

4. **extra** [more than usual; more than planned]

   We must take **extra** money on our trip.

   A: I thought you'd return from your vacation on Monday.
   B: We were having a lot of fun, so we decided to stay two **extra** days.

5. **casual** [not planned; not formal]

   You should wear **casual** clothes to a picnic.

   A: Some people don't like **casual** visits.
   B: I know. They like to know when friends plan to visit so that they can clean their house and prepare food.

6. **deserve** [should get]

   He **deserves** a vacation because he has been working very hard.

   A: Don't you think that Marian **deserves** a pay raise?
   B: Yes. She **deserves** a high salary because she works very hard and does a good job.

7. **endless** [having, or appearing to have, no end]

   We drove through **endless** miles of desert.

   A: I thought the train ride would never end.
   B: I know. It did appear to be **endless**.

8. **envy** [to want to have something that another person has]

   They were filled with **envy** when they saw the photographs of his vacation.

   A: Why are the children **envious** of Tim?
   B: Because Tim is going on an expensive vacation with his parents.

9. **equal** [the same in some way]

   People should receive **equal** pay for **equal** work!
   One and one **equals** two.

   A: We plan to divide the cost of our vacation **equally**.
   B: Maggie, Elizabeth, and I will each pay one third of the gas.

10. **expedition** [a long trip for studying or exploring]

    Mr. Jones went on an **expedition** to explore a South American jungle.

    A: Why did Joe go on a climbing **expedition**?
    B: Because he enjoys mountain climbing.

11. **intend** [to think of something as a purpose or plan]

    I **intend** to take a trip to China next year.

    A: Eric **intends** to visit his family in Germany this summer.
    B: I know. I **intend** to go with him.

12. **toward** [in the direction of something]

    We walked **toward** the ocean to watch the beautiful sunset.

    A: Do you know where Michael is?
    B: Yes. Walk **toward** the lake, and you'll find him fishing.

13. **procedure** [a method of doing something]

    What is the **procedure** for getting a driver's license?

    A: How can I get a visa to go to India?
    B: Call the Indian embassy and ask them to tell you the correct **procedure**.

14. **rise** [to come up or go up or get up]

> The sun **rises** in the east.
> The mountain **rose** 10,000 feet above them.

> A: What time will the sun **rise** tomorrow morning?
> B: Sunrise will occur at 6:30 tomorrow morning.

15. **rush** [to move very fast; to hurry]

> He **rushed** to the airport to meet his friend.
> They felt a **rush** of warm air.

> A: I had to **rush** to the train station this morning.
> B: Why?
> A: Because I got up late.

16. **whenever** [at any time, or every time]

> I smile **whenever** I think of our vacation in Spain.

> A: When can we leave?
> B: We can leave **whenever** you want to.

17. **sight** [something that someone sees; something pleasant or interesting to see]

> The **sight** of the ocean made me happy.

> A: Have you seen the **sights** of the city?
> B: Yes. We saw all the **sights** by bus yesterday.

18. **sunset** [when the sun does down (sets) at night]

> We saw many beautiful **sunsets** during the mountain climbing expedition.

> A: At what time will the sun **set** tonight?
> B: **Sunset** will occur at 8:00 tonight.

19. **view** [everything that can be seen from a certain place]

> The **view** of the forest from the top of the mountain was exciting.
> We **viewed** the mountains from the airplane.

> A: Do you know where I can go to get the best **view** of the city at night?
> B: The best **view** is from the top of the hill on the other side of the river.

Introductory Exercises

A. Match each word with its definition.

_____ 1. height
_____ 2. the same in some way
_____ 3. a method of doing something
_____ 4. used to
_____ 5. in the direction of something
_____ 6. a trip for studying or exploring
_____ 7. at any time
_____ 8. to be able to pay
_____ 9. to hurry
_____ 10. having no end
_____ 11. to go up
_____ 12. more than usual
_____ 13. not planned or formal

a. accustomed to
b. afford
c. altitude
d. casual
e. endless
f. envy
g. equal
h. expedition
i. extra
j. intend
k. procedure
l. rise
m. rush
n. toward
o. whenever

B. Substitute a word from the word form chart for the underlined word(s) in each sentence.

1. Look at all of the beautiful <u>parks and buildings</u>!
2. He's a good worker. He <u>should get</u> a vacation.
3. We both receive <u>the same</u> salary.
4. The trip appeared <u>to last forever</u>.
5. I <u>plan</u> to take a vacation in August.
6. She always brings <u>more than enough</u> clothes on vacation.
7. We can go home <u>any time</u> you wish.
8. The child ran <u>in the direction of</u> the lake.
9. The sun <u>came up</u> at 7:00 this morning.
10. Mr. Jones went on a <u>trip</u> to study plants in Canada.
11. He <u>hurried</u> to meet his friend at the hotel.

Study Exercises

C. Match the words that have similar meanings (synonyms).

____ **1.** hurry	**a.** altitude
____ **2.** method	**b.** equal
____ **3.** more	**c.** expedition
____ **4.** height	**d.** extra
____ **5.** same	**e.** intend
____ **6.** plan	**f.** procedure
____ **7.** scene	**g.** rush
____ **8.** trip	**h.** view

D. Write **T** if the sentence is true and **F** if it is false.

____ **1.** The width of a mountain is its altitude.

____ **2.** A procedure is a method of doing something.

____ **3.** You can afford a car when you have enough money to buy it.

____ **4.** You can see the sunset in the morning.

____ **5.** You walk slowly when you rush.

____ **6.** You wear casual clothes to a formal party.

____ **7.** An endless trip appears short.

____ **8.** People deserve a vacation if they work hard.

____ **9.** The sun rises early in the morning.

____ **10.** You envy your friend when you want something that he or she has.

____ **11.** A view is everything that you can see from a certain place.

E. In the blanks, write the appropriate word(s) from the word form chart in this unit.

1. They _____ to go home soon.

2. Bill walked _____ the pond.

3. The girls were _____ of Mary's new clothes.

4. We're _____ going to the ocean each summer.

5. She wears _____ clothes during her vacation.

6. I can't _____ to go on vacation. I don't have enough money.

7. My sister _____ -s early each morning.

8. I'm late! I have to _____ to the airport.

9. We saw many beautiful _____ during our vacation.

10. Mr. Smith works hard all day. He _____ -s to rest.

11. He had a nice _____ from his hotel room.

12. They receive _____ salaries.

13. I can't breathe well at high _____ -s .

14. The cave exploring _____ was exciting.

F. Circle the word which is different in meaning.

1. rush   rise   hurry

2. equal   envy   same

3. endless   forever   equal

4. view   procedure   method

5. expedition   rush   trip

6. altitude   height   last

7. sight   envy   want

G. Read the passage and answer the questions that follow.

Last summer Tom and his friends George and Bill wanted to take a vacation, but they did not have much money. They decided that a short mountain climbing expedition was the only trip they could afford. Since each of
5 them was accustomed to climbing, the vacation would be a lot of fun.

Tom made all the plans. He decided that they should share the expenses for food and gas equally and that each one should bring some extra clothes because the weather at high
10 altitudes is usually cold.

The boys were not in a hurry, so they climbed casually the first day. The weather was pleasant, and they enjoyed the fresh air as they climbed up a narrow path. Tom expected the weather to stay nice, but late in the afternoon there was a
15 storm. The boys rushed toward a cave and decided to camp there that night.

When the sun rose the next morning, they continued climbing. As the boys went higher, the climbing became more dangerous, and by late that afternoon the trip appeared
20 endless.

When they finally reached the top of the mountain, they saw a beautiful sight. The colors of the sunset were yellow,

red, and gold. The boys relaxed and enjoyed the view. The farms and fields of wheat and corn below appeared very
25 small. In the distance, they could see many trees, hills, and valleys.

Tom, George, and Bill spent four more days camping and exploring the mountains. When they returned from their vacation, they told their friend Jim about the fun they had
30 had. Jim was envious. He had intended to go with them, but he could not go at the last minute because he had to work. Jim told the boys that he wanted to go with them whenever they decided to go on another mountain climbing expedition.

Write **T** if the sentence is true and **F** if it is false.

_____ **1.** Tom, George, and Jim went on vacation together.
_____ **2.** A short mountain climbing expedition was the only vacation the boys could afford.
_____ **3.** Tom made all the plans.
_____ **4.** George paid for all the food and gas.
_____ **5.** The boys brought extra clothes because their other clothes would get dirty.
_____ **6.** The weather at high altitudes is usually cold.
_____ **7.** The boys camped in a cave the first night of their vacation.
_____ **8.** The weather was perfect during their vacation.
_____ **9.** The boys enjoyed the view from the top of the mountain.
_____ **10.** The vacation lasted five days.
_____ **11.** Bill was envious because he had intended to go on vacation with his friends.

Answer the questions.

1. Why did the boys bring extra clothes? _____

_____

2. What did the boys see when they finally reached the top of the

mountain? _____

_____

3. Why didn't Jim go mountain climbing with his friends? _____

_____

Follow-up

H. Dictation: Write the sentences that your teacher reads aloud.

1. _____

2. _____

3. _____

4. _____

5. _____

I. Answer each question with a word from the word form chart in this unit.

1. What kind of clothes do you wear on a picnic?
2. What are the interesting places you see on a trip?
3. What do you do when you're in a hurry?
4. What does warm air do?
5. What kind of trip do you go on to explore?
6. What do you see in the western part of the sky every evening?
7. What position are you in if you receive the worst grades in your class?
8. What is everything that you see from a certain place?
9. What must you follow correctly to get a driver's license?
10. How would some people feel if their best friend won a car?
11. Where are you going when you walk in the direction of something or someone?
12. What kind of trips appear to last forever?

J. Talk about one of the following subjects.

1. The most beautiful sights in your city or country.
2. An expedition you have taken.
3. A vacation you intend to take in the future.

Crime

Word Form Chart

NOUN	VERB	ADJECTIVE	ADVERB	PREPOSITION
action	act	acting		
actor				
actress				
				against
alert	alert	alert	alertly	
beggar	beg	begging		
blame	blame			
bother	bother	bothersome		
clue				
embarrassment	embarrass	embarrassed		
		embarrassing		
fault	fault			
forgiveness	forgive	forgiving		
	(forgave,			
	forgiven)			
human	human		humanly	
legality	legalize	legal	legally	
illegality		illegal	illegally	
poison	poison	poisonous		
		poisoned		
prison	imprison	imprisoned		
protection	protect	protective		
		protected		
safety	save	safe	safely	
scream	scream	screaming		
suicide		suicidal		

Definitions and Examples

1. **safe** [without danger]

    You should put your money in a **safe** place.
    Some areas of the city are not **safe** at night.
    A **safe** is a heavy box with a lock. You put money in it so that no
    one can steal it.

2. **suicide** [when a person kills himself]

    The unhappy man committed **suicide** by shooting himself.
    The police did not know if the death was murder or **suicide**.

3. **prison** [a jail]

    The murderer was sent to **prison** for life.
    No one wants to be in **prison**.

4. **poison** [a substance that can kill or hurt you if you eat or drink it]

    She committed suicide by drinking a **poison**.
    The murderer killed his victim with **poison**.
    Some plants are **poisonous**.

5. **action** [something that someone does]

    The police thought that the man's **actions** were strange, so they
    questioned him.
    That man is an **actor** on television.
    She is studying **acting** to become an **actress**.

6. **beg** [to ask with strong feeling for something you really need]

    Sometimes hungry people **beg** for food.
    The **beggars** in the street asked us for money.
    The students **begged** the teacher to give them an easy test.

7. **bother** [to make someone feel uncomfortable]

    The beggars **bothered** the rich tourists as they left their hotel.

    A: What **bothers** you most about living in a foreign country?
    B: Not understanding the language.

8. **human** [a person]

    Humans are more intelligent than animals.
    Humans use language, but animals cannot.

9. **protect** [to guard]

> The police try to **protect** us from criminals.
> Some people carry guns as **protection**.

10. **clue** [something that the police find which helps them solve a crime]

> The murderer left many **clues** at the scene of the crime.
> The investigators could not catch the robber because he left no **clues**.

11. **against** [not with; on the other side]

> The United States fought **against** Germany in World War II.
> The police protect us **against** crime.

12. **legal** [permitted by the law]

> Murder is not **legal**; it is **illegal**.
>
> A: What is the **legal** age to vote here?
> B: Eighteen.

13. **scream** [to use a loud, frightened voice]

> The woman **screamed** when the robbers attacked her.
> The baby **screamed** because he was hurt.

14. **blame** [to think or say that a person has done something bad]

> The police **blamed** the young man for the robbery and arrested him.
> The girl was **blamed** for the accident because she had been driving the car.

15. **embarrassment** [the feeling you have when you do something not intelligent in public]

> He felt great **embarrassment** when he could not remember his speech.
> She was **embarrassed** when the people laughed at her mistake.

16. **forgive** [to stop blaming a person for something bad which the person has done]

> The parents of the victim never **forgave** the drunk driver who killed their daughter.
> The boy begged his parents to **forgive** him for robbing the store.

17. **alert** [able to see or hear easily; very awake]

> Drivers must be **alert** when they drive in traffic.
> To avoid robberies, people should be very **alert**.

18. **fault** [the responsibility for a bad action]

    The bus driver was at **fault** in the accident.
    The broken window is my **fault**; my baseball hit it.

Introductory Exercises

A. Match each word with its definition.

_____ 1. permitted by the law

_____ 2. to ask people for money or food

_____ 3. able to see or hear easily

_____ 4. a substance that can kill you if you eat or drink it

_____ 5. a jail

_____ 6. a person

_____ 7. to guard

_____ 8. without danger

_____ 9. the responsibility for a bad action

_____ 10. to use a loud, frightened voice

_____ 11. to think or say that a person has done something wrong

_____ 12. to make someone feel uncomfortable

_____ 13. when a person kills himself

_____ 14. something that the police find which helps them solve a crime

a. action
b. against
c. alert
d. beg
e. blame
f. bother
g. clue
h. embarrass
i. fault
j. forgive
k. human
l. legal
m. poison
n. prison
o. protect
p. safe
q. scream
r. suicide

B. Complete each sentence with a word from the word form chart in this unit.

1. The judge sent the robber to _____ for ten years.

2. Driving too fast is _____ the law; it's illegal.

3. Putting your money in a safe will _____ it from robbers.

4. The victim of the attack _____-ed loudly.

5. Many people are _____ when they have to speak in front of a large group.

6. The old woman committed _____ because she did not want to live any longer.

7. The murderer killed his victim by putting _____ in his coffee.

8. John Wayne was a famous movie _____ .

9. The police had so many _____ that they easily found the criminal.

10. Animals are not _____ ; only people are.

Study Exercises

C. Write **T** if the sentence is true and **F** if it is false.

_____ 1. The victim of a murder is often blamed.

_____ 2. People like to be embarrassed.

_____ 3. People who are blamed for murders often go to prison.

_____ 4. People should do illegal things.

_____ 5. If you are well-protected, you are safe.

_____ 6. Screaming is a nice sound.

_____ 7. The police like to have a lot of clues.

_____ 8. Rich people often beg for money.

_____ 9. Actresses are often beautiful.

_____ 10. People do not like to be bothered.

_____ 11. An action which is against the law is legal.

D. Match each word with its opposite.

_____ 1. beggar
_____ 2. bother
_____ 3. embarrassed
_____ 4. forgive
_____ 5. poison
_____ 6. protect
_____ 7. safe
_____ 8. scream

a. blame
b. human
c. speak softly
d. rich person
e. comfortable
f. dangerous
g. medicine
h. hurt
i. make comfortable
j. suicide

E. Read the passage and answer the questions that follow.

The president of Honesty Bank, Mr. Henry Simms, was found dead yesterday in his office at the bank, a victim of suicide. Police investigating the death discovered that the bank's main safe had been robbed two days earlier.

5 The clues found in the bank showed that a group of robbers had entered the safe and taken almost all of the money, a total of about five million dollars.

Mr. Simms had discovered the robbery and knew that he would be blamed for losing the five million dollars because

10 he had not locked the safe. Unable to live with the embarrassment of not protecting the money, he poisoned himself.

Mr. Simms left a letter explaining what had happened and begging the forgiveness of the people whose money he

15 had not protected well enough.

1. How did Mr. Sims die? _____

_____

2. What part of the bank did the robbers take the money from? _____

_____

3. Why was Mr. Simms to blame for the robbery? _____

_____

4. How did Mr. Simms commit suicide? _____

_____

5. Why did he commit suicide? _____

_____

6. What did he beg for in his final letter? _____

_____

Follow-up

F.   Dictation: Write the sentences that your teacher reads aloud.

1. _____

2. _____

3. _____

4. _____

5. _____

G.   Answer the following questions.

1. Have you been embarrassed during the last week? Why?
2. Have you seen people begging? Where?
3. What bothers you in class? At home?
4. Have you ever been poisoned by accident? How?
5. Is there a prison in this city? Where?
6. Under what conditions is it illegal to drink beer here?
7. Which parts of this city are the safest?
8. Have you ever been blamed for something that you didn't do? Explain.
9. Who is your favorite actor? Actress?
10. When do you have to be very alert?

H.   Describe some methods people use to protect themselves against crime.

Science

Word Form Chart

NOUN	VERB	ADJECTIVE	ADVERB
acid		acidic	
atmosphere		atmospheric	
combination	combine	combined	
	crush	crushed	
	fill	filled	
		full	
geology		geological	
geologist			
inch	inch		
		incredible	incredibly
		marine	
mass		massive	
metal		metallic	
meter		metric	
powder	powder	powdered	
		powdery	
psychology		psychological	psychologically
psychologist			
questionnaire	question		
research	research		
researcher			
rocket			
technology		technological	technologically
technologist			
telescope		telescopic	
zero			

Definitions and Examples

1. **incredible** [difficult to believe]

   Fifty years ago the idea of travel to the moon was **incredible**.

   A: I got 100% on my math test.
   B: That's **incredible**. You didn't study!

2. **marine** [related to the ocean]

   A **marine** biologist studies the fish and other living things in the oceans.
   The **marine** life in parts of the oceans near large cities is being hurt by pollution.

3. **atmosphere** [the layer of gases which is around the earth]

   If the earth had no **atmosphere**, people could not breathe.
   We should be careful not to pollute our **atmosphere**.

4. **geology** [the study of the earth, the substances of which it is made, and its layers]

   My sister is majoring in **geology** in college. She is always looking at rocks.
   Geologists help the oil companies locate new oil.

5. **telescope** [an instrument used to look at distant objects]

   People use **telescopes** to study the stars and the moon.
   Scientists use large **telescopes** located in pollution-free areas to study the stars.

6. **zero** [no; none; 0]

   Water freezes at **zero** degrees Centigrade.
   He received a **zero** on the test because he did not answer any of the questions.

7. **crush** [to destroy something completely by pushing on it]

   The car was **crushed** in the accident; a bus pushed it into a wall.
   The mother **crushed** the pill and put it in the child's food so that he could eat it.

8. **metal** [a substance from the earth that is shiny]

   Cars are made mostly of **metals**.
   Gold is a **metal**.

9. **mass** (a) [some material that stays together in one piece]

    It is difficult to lift a large **mass** of water.

    (b) [how much material is present in an object]

    The **mass** of something is related to its weight.

    (c) [a large number or large group]

    A **mass** of humanity pushed in the direction of the train.
    Mass production requires many workers.

10. **massive** [very large; very heavy]

    The Titanic was a **massive** ship.
    A **massive** rock blocked the street.

11. **psychology** [the study of how people think and why they do the things they do]

    Many college students take a course in **psychology**.
    Some **psychologists** investigate why some people become criminals.

12. **research** [investigation with the purpose of increasing our knowledge in some area, for example science or education]

    Some psychologists do **research** on why people may become
      criminals.
    My sister is **researching** the marine life off the coast of California.

13. **powder** [a solid which is in very small and fine pieces]

    The machine crushed the stone into a **powder**.
    Powered milk can be stored for a long time.

14. **combine** [to put two or more things together]

    If you **combine** powdered milk and water, you get liquid milk.
    Some metals are a **combination** of other metals.

15. **fill** [to put a liquid or solid into a box, bag, glass, etc. until no more can fit in]

    My mother **filled** my plate with food.
    The box was **filled** with old clothes.

16. **questionnaire** [a group of questions used to get information for research purposes]

    Psychologists often use **questionnaires** in their research.
    The **questionnaire** had a total of one hundred questions.

17. **metric** [based on the meter, a measurement used in most parts of the world]

> In 1986 the United States was still using English measurement, not **metric** measurement.
> Kilograms are a **metric** measure.
> The **metric** system is the system of measurement used in most parts of the world.

18. **inch** [part of the English system of measurement, about 2.5 centimeters]

> My left foot is seven **inches** long.
> There are twelve **inches** in a foot in the English system of measurement.

19. **rocket** [a machine similar to an airplane, which can reach the space outside the earth's atmosphere]

> **Rockets** use a lot of fuel.
> **Rockets** were first used during World War II.
> A **rocket** took Neil Armstrong to the moon in 1969.

20. **technology** [the use of science in industry]

> **Technology** helps make our lives easier.
> The use of **technology** has increased a lot in the last twenty years.

21. **acid** [one of a group of liquids that in their strong form will burn you if you touch them]

> Some **acids** can burn through metals.
> Weak **acids** are in some fruits.

Introductory Exercises

A. Match each word with its definition.

_____ 1. 2.5 centimeters
_____ 2. to put two or more things together
_____ 3. a solid which is in very small pieces
_____ 4. the study of the earth
_____ 5. 0
_____ 6. the study of how people think and act
_____ 7. a group of questions used to get information for research purposes
_____ 8. a machine which can reach the space outside the earth's atmosphere
_____ 9. some material in one piece
_____ 10. to destroy something completely
_____ 11. an instrument used to look at distant places
_____ 12. a substance from the earth, usually shiny
_____ 13. related to the ocean
_____ 14. to put a liquid or solid into a box, glass, etc. until no more can fit in
_____ 15. difficult to believe
_____ 16. the layer of gases which is around the earth

a. acid
b. atmosphere
c. combine
d. crush
e. fill
f. geology
g. inch
h. incredible
i. marine
j. mass
k. metal
l. metric
m. powder
n. psychology
o. questionnaire
p. research
q. rocket
r. technology
s. telescope
t. zero

B. Answer each question with a word from the word form chart in this unit.

1. What do scientists do?
2. Who helps locate oil?
3. What is around the earth?
4. What is something that you cannot believe?
5. What do you use to look at the moon?
6. What number is less than one?
7. What do psychologists often use in their research?
8. What are gold and silver?
9. What's the opposite of "empty"?

10. What is used to go to the moon?
11. What do you have after you crush a stone?
12. What type of life is in the oceans?
13. What system of measurement is used in France?
14. Who studies people's thoughts and actions?
15. What can burn through metal?

Study Exercises

C. Write **T** if the sentence is true and **F** if it is false.

_____ **1.** Geologists study the fish in the ocean.

_____ **2.** A heavy car has a lot of mass.

_____ **3.** Parts of rockets are made of metal.

_____ **4.** Cooks often combine foods when they cook.

_____ **5.** You can eat strong acids.

_____ **6.** Humans can breathe the earth's atmosphere.

_____ **7.** An inch is longer than a mile.

_____ **8.** People use rockets for transportation in cities.

_____ **9.** Some medicines are in the form of powders.

_____ **10.** A psychologist studies rocks.

_____ **11.** There was lot of technology 300 years ago.

_____ **12.** You can put more water in a full glass.

_____ **13.** A telescope is an example of technology.

D. Circle the word which is different in meaning.

1. mass   geologist   psychologist
2. inch   mile   telescope
3. research   zero   million
4. metal   metric   brick
5. acid   massive   large
6. rocket   airplane   geology
7. powder   telescope   liquid
8. crush   destroy   fill

E. In the blanks, write the appropriate word from the word form chart in this unit.

1. The robber used _____ to burn through the metal around the lock of the safe.

2. My uncle has been doing _____ on marine life for more than twenty years.

3. Elephants are _____ animals.

4. Fish are an example of _____ life.

5. As part of his research, the psychologist asked many people to answer the questions on his _____ .

6. The idea for the number _____ came from the Arabs; Roman numbers didn't have this idea.

7. Airplanes are not able to reach the end of the earth's atmosphere, but _____ can.

8. When the elephant stepped on the box, the box was

_____ .

9. The little girl did not want to take the pill, so her mother crushed it into a _____ and put it in her food.

10. The two main ways of measuring are using English measures and _____ measures.

11. That story about a talking horse was _____ .

Follow-up

F. Dictation: Write the sentences that your teacher reads aloud.

1. _____

2. _____

3. _____

4. _____

5. _____

G. Answer the following questions.

1. Have you used a telescope? What did you look at?
2. Name a food combination that is usual in your country.
3. Have you been to a marine zoo? What did you see?
4. What is the most massive building in your city?
5. Name some recent technological advances.
6. Do you know the names in English of any metals other than gold? What are they?
7. Do you know the names in English of any foods which are acidic? What are they?
8. How tall are you in inches?

H. Compare the work of a psychologist to the work of a geologist.

Weather/Geography

Word Form Chart

NOUN	VERB	ADJECTIVE	ADVERB
aridity		arid	
climate		climatic	
continent		continental	
harshness		harsh	harshly
hemisphere		hemispheric	
humidity	humidify	humid	
	ignore		
inclusion	include	included	
		inclusive	
island			
lightning			
	mind		
orange		orange	
reluctance		reluctant	reluctantly
seriousness		serious	seriously
severity		severe	severely
shade	shade	shady	
shaded			
		temperate	
thunder	thunder	thunderous	
	wet	wet	
zone	zone	zoning	
		zoned	

Definitions and Examples

1. **climate** [the type of weather in general in a large area]

    The **climate** in North America is not too hot in summer and not too cold in winter.

    A: I come from a very cold **climate**. Snow doesn't bother me.
    B: I come from a warm **climate**. I've never seen snow before!

2. **temperate** [with weather that is not too hot and not too cold]

    I like **temperate** climates best.

    A: Is the weather in Tahiti **temperate**?
    B: No. It's tropical.

3. **wet** [having water on or in]

    When it rains, the streets and buildings get all **wet**.

    A: Did you bring your umbrella today? It's going to rain.
    B: Oh, no! I forgot! I'm going to get **wet** on the way home.

4. **humid** [having wet air]

    Humid climates are not dry.

    A: It feels so hot and **humid** today. We shouldn't go to the park.
    B: It feels hotter when it's **humid** like this.

5. **arid** [very dry]

    A climate that is **arid** usually doesn't have many plants.

    A: I prefer **arid** climates to humid ones.
    B: Not me. I don't like dry, arid climates.

6. **thunder** [a loud noise during a rainstorm]

    Thunder frightens some people.

    A: Did you hear that loud **thunder**? It sounded near.
    B: Yes. It will rain soon.

7. **lightning** [the electricity in the sky during a rainstorm]

    Thunder and **lightning** usually come at the same time.

    A: I hate thunderstorms.
    B: Me too. I'm always afraid that the **lightning** will hit our house.

8. **harsh** [difficult; hard]

   A **harsh** climate is one in which the weather is very hot or very
   cold.

   A: Does Australia have a **harsh** climate?
   B: Only in some places.

9. **hemisphere** [half of a completely round object]

   We can divide the earth into two **hemispheres**:
   the northern and the southern.

   A: Is Peru in the northern **hemisphere**?
   B: No! Where did you learn geography?

10. **continent** [a large body of land]

    There are seven **continents**: Europe, Asia, North America, South
    America, Africa, Australia, and Antarctica.

    A: Do you think that there are seven **continents**?
    B: Yes. But some people think there are only five: Europe, Asia,
    America, Australia, and Africa.

11. **include** [to add someone or something to a group]

    Do you **include** South America as a continent?

    A: I like all kinds of weather, **including** rain!
    B: You're strange.

12. **ignore** [to leave someone out of a group; not to pay attention to
    someone or something]

    I never **ignore** my friends, even if they are doing something I do not
    like.

    A: This humid weather really makes me feel tired.
    B: Just **ignore** it and try to enjoy your vacation!

13. **mind** [to be bothered by something]

    Do you **mind** the cold in winter?

    A: I don't **mind** rain, but I prefer sunny weather.
    B: Rain doesn't bother me either.

14. **orange** [a color between yellow and red]

    When the sun is almost down, the sky and clouds are **orange** and
    pink.

    A: Where are we going? I'm lost.
    B: Look at the **orange** sign. It says, "Food and gas, 2 miles."

15. **shady** [not sunny]

> We have many trees near our house so it's **shady** and cool in the summer.

> A: Do you prefer to walk in the sun or in the **shade**?
> B: It's too hot in the sun. We should walk on the **shady** path.

16. **severe** [harsh]

> The weather in Antarctica is **severely** cold.

> A: The teacher made us stay one hour after class to finish our homework.
> B: That was very **severe**.

17. **serious** [not funny; important]

> His illness was **serious**; he might have died.

> Teacher A: I'm **serious**. Don't be late to class again!
> Student B: I'm sorry.

18. **reluctant** [not wanting to do something]

> He appears **reluctant** to move to England. He really does not want to go.

> A: Do you want to go to China with me?
> B: I'm **reluctant** to say "yes." I don't have enough money, and I'm not sure I will like it.

19. **island** [land with water all around it]

> Australia is a large **island**.

> A: Would you like to live on an **island**?
> B: No. I can't swim, and I don't like fishing.

20. **zone** [area]

> There are three major **zones** in the northern hemisphere: the Arctic **zone**, the temperate **zone**, and the tropical **zone**.

> A: Do you live in the business **zone** of your city?
> B: No. I live in the residential **zone**.

Introductory Exercises

A. Match each word with its definition.

    ____ 1. wet air

    ____ 2. difficult; hard

    ____ 3. a large body of land

    ____ 4. not to pay attention

    ____ 5. not sunny

    ____ 6. a loud noise

    ____ 7. to be bothered by something

    ____ 8. half of a round object

    ____ 9. electricity in the sky

    ____ 10. dry

    ____ 11. with weather that is not too
hot and not too dry

a. arid
b. continent
c. harsh
d. hemisphere
e. humidity
f. ignore
g. island
h. lightning
i. mind
j. serious
k. shady
l. temperate
m. thunder

B. Complete the sentence with a word from the word form chart in this unit.

1. A hot, dry climate is also called an _____ climate.

2. Before it rains, the air is usually _____ .

3. I like to sit under the trees because it is cool and _____ .

4. If it rains, you'll get _____ .

5. When you have a _____ accident, you have to go to the hospital.

6. The weather in Antarctica can be described as _____
   or _____ .

7. At sunset, the sky is red, yellow, and _____ .

8. Janet walked past me and didn't say hello. She
   _____ -ed me.

9. _____ and _____ are usually part of a severe
   rainstorm.

10. Large bodies of land are called _____ .

11. The northern _____ has oceans and several continents.

Study Exercises

C. Write **T** if the sentence is true and **F** if it is false.

_____ **1.** Islands are lakes in the middle of continents.

_____ **2.** Orange is a color.

_____ **3.** Shady is the same as humid.

_____ **4.** Severe thunderstorms are very bad thunderstorms.

_____ **5.** If you live in a harsh climate, it is difficult to be outside all the time.

_____ **6.** Thunder can frighten people if it is very loud.

_____ **7.** Geography includes the study of land, islands, oceans, rivers, and continents.

_____ **8.** An arid climate is the same as a wet climate.

_____ **9.** Most people do not mind harsh weather.

_____ **10.** Most people hate temperate climates.

_____ **11.** A broken leg is not very serious.

_____ **12.** Lightning is what you do to the house when it is dark.

_____ **13.** It is possible to ignore the rain if you are inside.

D. Match each word with its opposite.

_____ **1.** arid

_____ **2.** severe

_____ **3.** wet

_____ **4.** shady

_____ **5.** wanting to

_____ **6.** serious

_____ **7.** ignore

a. funny
b. humid
c. harsh
d. happy
e. dry
f. sunny
g. nice
h. reluctant to
i. include

E. Fill in the blanks with a word from the word form chart in this unit.

Inge was (1) _____ to move to Alaska from Germany. She had heard the weather was (2) _____ there. Not only was it (3) _____ cold in the winter, but it was cool in the summer, too. Inge did not (4) _____ a cold climate, but she had never seen rainstorms like the ones in Alaska! The (5) _____ and (6) _____ were terrible! Afterward, the whole city was (7) _____ and (8) _____ for

days. but the sunsets were beautiful. the deep reds and
(9) _____ -s were a lovely sight. Finally, Inge grew
accustomed to her life on a new (10) _____ .

F.   Read the passage and answer the questions that follow.

       Saudi Arabia and Bolivia are very different countries in
many ways. They both have harsh environments, but they
are harsh for different reasons.

       The major part of Saudi Arabia, in the Middle East, is
5 arid, flat land. It receives very little rain and has only a few
small rivers. There are very few plants in the desert area of
Saudi Arabia. Those plants are near oases, or water holes. But
in the true desert no one can live. Even the desert people
who live on oases avoid the terrible sand and rock hills.
10 Neither water nor food can be found in the true Arabian
desert.

       Bolivia, an interior country of South America, has its
own harsh climate. Much of Bolivia is tropical lowlands.
Almost no one lives in these lowlands because of the daily,
15 heavy rains, many floods, and very humid air that is difficult
to breathe. The yearly rainfall in Bolivia is between 40 and
60 inches. Even so, there are not many usable plants in the
tropical lowlands of Bolivia. Most of the area is covered with
grass that is not even good for animals to eat.

1. Where is Saudi Arabia? _____

_____

2. What kind of climate does it have? _____

_____

3. Where can some plants grow in the desert? _____

_____

4. What is the land like in the true desert? _____

_____

5. Can you find food or water there? _____

_____

6. Where is Bolivia? _____

_____

7. What kind of climate does it have? _____

_____

8. Why doesn't anyone live in the lowlands? _____

_____

9. How much rain falls in Bolivia? _____

_____

10. What kinds of plants are there in Bolivia? _____

_____

Follow-up

G. Dictation: Write the sentences that your teacher reads aloud.

1. _____

2. _____

3. _____

4. _____

5. _____

H. Answer the following questions.

    1. Do you live in a humid area or an arid area?
    2. Which hemisphere are we in now? Have you visited other hemispheres?
    3. Are you afraid of thunder? Lightning?
    4. Do you mind humid weather? What do you do when the weather is very humid?
    5. Is the climate in your area harsh? In what way(s) is it harsh?
    6. What is the name of your continent? Have you visited other continents?
    7. Do you like the color orange?
    8. Name the continents.
    9. Do you prefer sun or shade? Why?

I.   **1.** Describe your continent's weather.
     2. Describe the type of weather you like the best.
     3. Describe the worst storm you can remember.

Recreation

Word Form Chart

NOUN	VERB	ADJECTIVE	ADVERB
activity		active	actively
balloon			
	burst (burst, burst)	burst	
ceremony		ceremonious	ceremoniously
		ceremonial	ceremonially
	consist		
fantasy	fantasize		
		fantastic	fantastically
fool	fool	foolish	foolishly
foolishness			
fountain			
ghost		ghostly	
glue	glue	glued	
magic		magical	magically
magician			
		mental	mentally
model	model	model	
nightmare		nightmarish	nightmarishly
		numerous	
physique		physical	physically
		shallow	
slide	slide (slid, slid)	sliding	
smoothness	smooth	smooth	smoothly

Definitions and Examples

1. **activity** [something to do]

    People enjoy many different **activities** in their free time.

    A: What kinds of **activities** did they have at the picnic?
    B: They had games and contests for the children, but the older people only talked.

2. **physical** [with or of the body]

    People should get a lot of **physical** activity to stay healthy.
    That old man is not strong enough for that kind of **physical** work; he will hurt his back.

3. **balloon** [a thing that is filled with air and may rise up]

    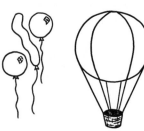

    The child received a big red **balloon** at the party.
    Riding in hot air **balloons** is a popular activity at our yearly city party.

4. **glue** [a substance used to stick one thing to another]

    The children used **glue** to put the blue paper on the wall.
    She used white **glue** to repair the broken chair leg.

5. **fountain** [a device that shoots water into the air]

    The **fountain** in the park is very beautiful.
    He stopped at the water **fountain** in the hall to get a drink.

6. **burst** [to break; to explode]

    The child screamed when the balloon **burst**.
    The children **burst** into laughter at the party.

7. **foolish** [without thinking; mistaken; stupid]

    She was **foolish** to build the fire near the dry trees.
    Driving fast under dangerous road conditions is **foolish**.

8. **shallow** [not deep]

    The children had to stay in the **shallow** end of the swimming pool.
    He lost the race because he caught his foot in a **shallow** hole and fell down.

9. **numerous** [many]

    They had **numerous** activities planned for the party.
    There were **numerous** children that we did not know.

10. **nightmare** [a frightening dream; a bad experience]

    The scary movie caused her to have **nightmares**.
    The party was a **nightmare**. Children jumped on the furniture, broke a window; and got the floors all dirty.

11. **smooth** [having a nice surface]

    Glass is **smooth**.
    The surface of the water looked **smooth**.
    The stones that the children walked on were very **smooth**.

12. **ceremony** [actions done according to a formal plan at a special time]

    The **ceremony** at the beginning of our neighborhood picnic is always the same. Old Mr. Jones stands up to talk about the accomplishments of the people, the band plays several songs, and the school children have a parade down Main Street.
    Their wedding **ceremony** was long but very beautiful.

13. **magic** [the doing of acts which usually seem impossible]

    My father can do a lot of **magic**. He can tell you which number you are thinking of. He can make things disappear. He can make a bird appear from nowhere. Of course, it's not really **magic**; he simply makes you think you are seeing these things happen.

14. **consist** (of) [to be made of]

    The picnic dinner **consisted of** chicken, salad, vegetables, cake, and drinks.
    The ceremony **consisted** of several speeches, some music, and a film.

15. **fantasy** [ideas that are not real; imagination]

    His biggest **fantasy** is to fly like a bird.
    Her story was so **fantastic** that we couldn't believe it.

16. **fantastic** [very good; wonderful]

    Our vacation was **fantastic**; we plan to go to the same place next year.

17. **mental** [related to thoughts or ideas in your head]

    While he was telling me about his travels, I made **mental** pictures of the places he was describing.
    He is not physically ill, but he does have some serious **mental** problems.

18. **slide** [to move smoothly over a surface; to almost fall down]

The children **slid** down the hill on the snow.
During the race, he **slid** on the grass, so another runner won.
Our favorite activity is to run and **slide** into the water.

19. **model** [an example of something in a smaller size; a type]

He likes to build wooden **models**. He has a **model** of an airplane,
   models of many kinds of cars, and **models** of buildings such as
   the Eiffel Tower and the Empire State Building.
He bought a **model** of the White House.

A: What **model** of car did he finally buy?
B: He got a 1986 Volkswagen Rabbit.

20. **ghost** [according to the belief of some people, the part of a person that
is not physical and leaves the body when he dies]

My cousin loves to tell stories of **ghosts** returning to houses to
   make noises and scare people.
She screamed because she thought she saw a **ghost** sliding down the
   stairs.
They believe that they can communicate with the **ghosts** of people
   who died hundreds of years ago.

Introductory Exercises

A. Match each word with its definition.

_____ **1.** a device that shoots water
into the air

_____ **2.** of the body

_____ **3.** a person who can make
things disappear

_____ **4.** to move smoothly

_____ **5.** related to thoughts or ideas

_____ **6.** a small example of something

_____ **7.** to break

_____ **8.** anything that you do

_____ **9.** to be made of; include

_____ **10.** unthoughtful; stupid

_____ **11.** not deep

_____ **12.** to create dreams, ideas, or
unreal thoughts

a. activity
b. burst
c. ceremony
d. consist of
e. fantasize
f. foolish
g. fountain
h. magician
i. mental
j. model
k. physical
l. shallow
m. slide
n. smooth

B.   Describe the activities or situations in the pictures.

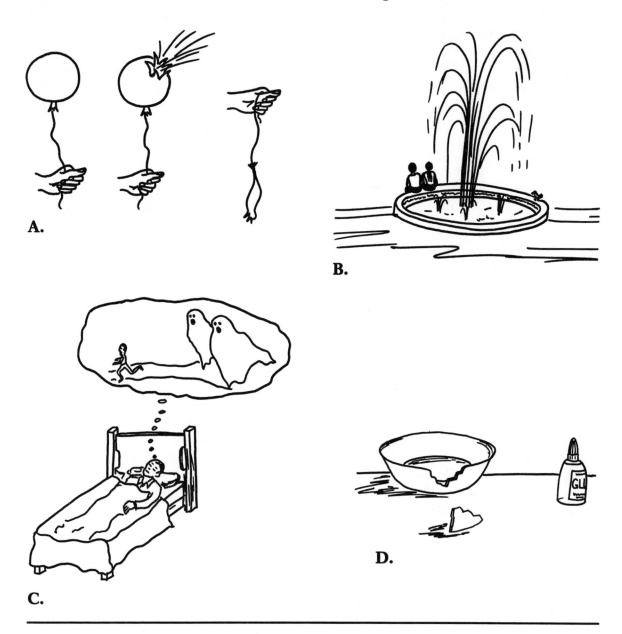

A.

B.

C.

D.

Study Exercises

C.   In the blanks, write the appropriate word(s) from the word form chart in this unit.

1. Physical _____ keeps your body strong.

2. The child woke up screaming because she had a(n)

    _____ .

3. The ballet dancer moved _____ across the floor.

4. Thinking is a(n) _____ activity; running is a(n) _____ activity.

5. People who cannot swim should stay in _____ water.

6. There were many people at the party; they were too _____ to count.

7. If you sit on a balloon, it will _____ .

8. His biggest _____ is to become rich and famous.

9. She does not like _____ stories because they frighten her.

10. The magician could not pick the box up, so he _____ it across the floor instead.

D. Describe the pictures in Exercise B.

1. (Picture A) _____

_____

2. (Picture B) _____

_____

3. (Picture C) _____

_____

4. (Picture D) _____

_____

E. Write **T** if the sentence is true and **F** if it is false.

_____ 1. Children frequently fantasize when they play.

_____ 2. Most living rooms have fountains in the corner.

_____ 3. There are numerous words on this page.

_____ 4. Glass is a very smooth material.

_____ 5. You can move heavy items by sliding them.

_____ 6. Ghosts are nightmarish to experience.

_____ 7. Shallow water is deep and very cold.

_____ 8. People enjoy having nightmares.

_____ 9. People use glue to build model airplanes.

_____ 10. A fool is a very intelligent person.

F.   Read the passages and answer the questions that follow.

> In the summer, there are always numerous outdoor activities and ceremonies in our city. We have movies in West Park every weekend and live music and theater outside in East Park on Monday evenings and Thursday evenings.
> 5   Frequently, magicians perform magic for everyone's entertainment and enjoyment.
>   For children, there are creative activities that they can take part in during the day. They can go to numerous locations around the city to learn to paint pictures, make
> 10   wooden models, sing international songs, etc. They can also get physical exercise in tennis classes, ballet classes, or sports clubs. If it is mental activity they are looking for, the children can take a three-week academic class in science, writing, reading, or mathematics. The city offers enough
> 15   activities for the children to stay busy all summer.

1. What does this city offer its people in the summer? _____

_____

2. What kinds of outdoor entertainment are there? _____

_____

3. What can children do during the day? _____

_____

4. Where can they go to learn various skills? _____

_____

5. What kinds of physical exercise are available? _____

_____

6. What kind of activity do the academic classes give them? _____

_____

> This past summer our city got a new fountain in the downtown area for its 200th anniversary. The fountain was made by several famous artists from around the world and shows our city's accomplishments over the last 200 years.
> 5   The water shoots high up from the center of the fountain and falls into a shallow area where lights shine through the water. To present the fountain to the public, the mayor

planned an official evening ceremony, consisting of speeches, music, and other entertainment. He gave a short speech and
10 introduced the artists, who spoke about the making and importance of the fountain. A band played loud music and thousands of balloons rose into the air as the mayor turned the water on. The crowd enjoyed the beauty of the fountain in the evening light and stayed downtown to continue
15 listening to music and watching other anniversary activities.

7. What did the city get this past summer and why? _____

_____

8. What does the fountain look like? _____

_____

9. How did the mayor present the fountain to the public? _____

_____

10. What did the ceremony consist of? _____

_____

11. What happened as the mayor turned on the water? _____

_____

12. Why did the people stay downtown? _____

_____

Follow-up

G. Dictation: Write the sentences that your teacher reads aloud.

1. _____

2. _____

3. _____

4. _____

5. _____

I. Answer the following questions.

1. What are some typical summer activities in your country? Winter? Indoor? Outdoor?
2. What are your favorite activities?
3. What kind of ceremonies have you gone to in the past year?
4. What is the difference between a nighmare and a fantasy? What is your biggest fantasy? Your scariest nightmare?
5. What is glue used for?
6. What is some typical magic that magicians perform?
7. How do you feel about ghosts? Are they real? Have you seen any, or are they just imagined?
8. When could someone be called a fool? In other words, how does a fool act?

J. Describe a ceremony which is typical of a special time in your country, town, or neighborhood.

Banking

Word Form Chart

NOUN	VERB	ADJECTIVE	ADVERB
accuracy		accurate	accurately
blank		blank	blankly
check		checking	
computer	computerize	computerized	
credit	credit	credited	
decrease	decrease	decreasing	decreasingly
		decreased	
down payment	pay . . . down		
maximum	maximize	maximum	maximally
minimum	minimize	minimum	minimally
	owe		
preciousness		precious	
rate			
repayment	repay (repaid, repaid)	repaid	
silver		silver	
subtraction	subtract	subtracted	
withdrawal	withdraw (withdrew, withdrawn)	withdrawn	

Definitions and Examples

1. **silver** [a metal often used to make coins]

   American quarters contain a lot of **silver**.
   Expensive knives and forks are sometimes made of **silver**.

2. **decrease** [to become smaller; to make smaller]

> I have spent a lot of money this week, so the amount of money in
>   my account has **decreased**.
> No one wants the interest his money earns to **decrease**.

3. **repay** [to pay back money which you have borrowed]

> He lent me $100, but I have to **repay** him by next week.
> After two years, they finally **repaid** all the money that they had
>   borrowed.

4. **withdraw** [to take money out of a bank account]

> She **withdrew** a large amount of money in order to buy a car.
> The old man was robbed soon after he had made a **withdrawal** from
>   his account.

5. **owe** [to need to repay money that you have borrowed]

> I **owe** the bank $500, which I borrowed last month.
>
> A: How much do you **owe** him?
> B: One hundred dollars plus interest.

6. **rate** [how fast or how much]

> That bank's interest **rate** for borrowing money is fifteen percent.
>
> A: What kind of interest does that account pay?
> B: The current **rate** is seven percent.

7. **check** [a form of payment by signed papers that people
with bank accounts can use]

> Not all stores will accept **checks**.
> I receive my salary each month in the form of a **check**.

8. **blank** [with nothing written on it]

> It is dangerous to give someone a **blank** check because the person
>   can write any amount of money on it.
> On the test we had to write one word in each **blank**.

9. **computer** [a technologically advanced machine which can use and give
information very rapidly]

> Banks often use **computers** because they have to do a lot of math.
> **Computers** can work much faster than humans.

10. **credit** [a way of paying for a purchase in which you pay a small part of the total each month]

> When you buy on **credit**, you usually have to pay interest and your monthly payment.
> People who already owe a lot of money usually cannot get **credit**.
> He used a **credit** card to make the purchase.

11. **down payment** [the amount of money you must pay at the beginning when you buy something on credit]

> The **down payment** on their house was $10,000.
>
> A: How much was the **down payment** on your new car?
> B: Only $500.

12. **minimum** [the smallest amount]

> The **minimum** down payment for a house in the United States is often ten percent.
> The **minimum** amount of money you need to open an account at that bank is ten dollars.

13. **accurate** [correct; without any errors]

> Bank clerks must be very **accurate** in their work.
> This bill is not **accurate**! It is for ten dollars too much.

14. **maximum** [the most; the highest; the largest number or amount]

> The **maximum** amount of interest you will get now is ten percent.
> The **maximum** speed permitted on this road is 55 miles per hour.

15. **precious** [of great value]

> Gold and silver are **precious** metals.
> Rings are often made with **precious** stones in them.

16. **subtract** [to take away]

> If you **subtract** 10 from 100, you get 90.
> Children learn addition and **subtraction** in elementary school.

Introductory Exercises

A. Match each word with its definition.

_____ **1.** with nothing written on it

_____ **2.** to pay back money which you have borrowed

_____ **3.** a metal often used to make coins

_____ **4.** a form of payment used instead of cash

_____ **5.** the smallest amount

_____ **6.** correct; without any errors

_____ **7.** to take away

_____ **8.** a machine which can use and give information very rapidly

_____ **9.** of great value

_____ **10.** to become smaller; to make smaller

_____ **11.** to need to repay money that you have borrowed

_____ **12.** to take money out of a bank account

_____ **13.** the largest amount

a. accurate
b. blank
c. computer
d. credit
e. decrease
f. down payment
g. maximum
h. minimum
i. owe
j. precious
k. rate
l. repay
m. silver
n. subtract
o. withdraw
p. check

B. Answer each question with a word from the word form chart in this unit.

1. What metal is precious?
2. What can you use if you do not want to pay in cash? (two answers)
3. What's the opposite of "addition"?
4. What machine can do math very fast?
5. What is a check before you write on it?
6. What do you do when you take money from a bank?
7. When you buy something on credit, what is the money that you pay at the beginning?
8. What are you doing when you pay back money that you owe?
9. How do you want your banker to do math?

Study Exercises

C. Write **T** if the sentence is true and **F** if it is false.

_____ 1. You want a high rate of interest when you borrow money.

_____ 2. People often buy houses on credit.

_____ 3. People give stores blank checks.

_____ 4. High school students study subtraction.

_____ 5. Many banks use computers.

_____ 6. When you buy on credit, a down payment is often required.

_____ 7. Gold is not a precious metal.

_____ 8. A person who adds accurately makes mistakes.

_____ 9. When you owe someone money, you should repay him.

_____ 10. People withdraw money from their bank accounts when they want to make a purchase.

_____ 11. People want to maximize the interest they receive.

D. Match each word with its opposite.

_____ 1. accurate

_____ 2. decrease

_____ 3. maximum

_____ 4. precious

_____ 5. repay

_____ 6. subtract

_____ 7. withdraw

a. without value
b. borrow
c. down payment
d. minimum
e. increase
f. put in
g. with errors
h. check
i. add

E. Read the passage and answer the questions that follow.

The United States is truly the land of the credit card. Americans use credit cards to buy almost everything. The use of credit cards has many important advantages. First, the use of cash is minimized, which means a decrease in
5 robberies. In addition, people can carry their credit cards and use them instead of making withdrawals of cash from their accounts. People can also place orders for purchases by phone and pay by giving their credit card number. This is easier and faster than paying by check.
10 However, the use of credit cards also has disadvantages for many Americans. If a credit card owner does not pay all

of the money that he owes at the end of the month, he is
really borrowing the money, but the rate of interest he must
pay on this borrowed money, until he repays all of it, is very
15 high—often about twenty percent. Because no down
payment is required for credit card purchases (no payment is
required until one month after the purchase, when the bill
arrives), many Americans have trouble limiting their
purchases. When the bills finally arrive, they see that they do
20 not have enough money. The result is high interest
payments.

1. Give three advantages of using credit cards.

    a. _____

    b. _____

    c. _____

2. Why should a person try to pay all of his credit card bill each

    month? _____

    _____

3. Why do some people have trouble limiting their credit card

    purchases? _____

    _____

Follow-up

F. Dictation: Write the sentences that your teacher reads aloud.

    1. _____

    2. _____

    3. _____

    4. _____

    5. _____

G.   Answer the following questions.

1. Who uses computers in your country?
2. When do people in your country use checks?
3. Has the cost of living in your country increased or decreased in the last year?
4. To buy a house in your country, what percent down payment is required?
5. What interest rate do banks in your country pay on savings accounts? What rate do they receive when they lend money?
6. Have you ever borrowed money? At what rate of interest? How long did it take you to repay the money?
7. What things are made of silver?
8. Do you think using credit cards is a good idea? Why or why not?

H.   Describe the forms of payment that people in your country use for the following:

1. buying a house
2. buying a car
3. buying food

Family

Word Form Chart

NOUN	VERB	ADJECTIVE	ADVERB	CONJUNCTION
adult		adult		
adulthood				
				although
approval	approve	approving	approvingly	
disapproval	disapprove	disapproving	disapprovingly	
anger	anger	angry	angrily	
beard		bearded		
behavior	behave	well-behaved		
	misbehave	misbehaving		
belongings	belong			
blond		blond		
bride		bridal		
conversation	converse	conversational	conversationally	
discussion	discuss			
emotion		emotional	emotionally	
independence		independent	independently	
dependence	depend	dependent	dependently	
		dependable	dependably	
		undependable		
infant		infantile		
infancy				
jealousy		jealous	jealously	
kiss	kiss			
	let (let, let)			
	ought to			
reliance	rely	reliable	reliably	
		reliant		

Definitions and Examples

1. **belong** (to) (a) [to be a part of]

   My whole family **belongs to** the City Health Club.

   (b) [to be owned by]

   A: Which of these things **belong to** you?
   B: None of them. They are all my sister's **belongings**.

2. **blond** [very light-colored hair]

   All of my sisters have **blond** hair, but my brothers have dark hair.
   The summer sun makes my hair even **blonder**.

3. **bride** [a woman who is going to get or has recently gotten married]

   The **bride** was very nervous right before her wedding ceremony.
   The **bride** wore a long white dress and had flowers in her hair.

4. **behavior** [how someone acts]

   Our children generally **behave** well when we take them out to
   dinner.
   If we **misbehaved** when we were children, we had to sit on a chair
   in the corner.

5. **infant** [a baby younger than one year old]

   Infants require a lot of attention.
   My sister has a twelve-year-old son and an **infant** girl.
   This man's **infantile** behavior is causing trouble for all of us.

6. **emotion** [how a person feels]

   Her **emotions** change so much! Sometimes she is happy, but
   sometimes very sad.
   Love is an **emotion** necessary for good health.

7. **let** [to permit]

   We never **let** our children stay up too late when they have school
   the next day.
   When we were young, our parents never **let** us eat a lot of sugar.

8. **beard** [the hair on a man's face]

   My brother had to cut off his **beard** before he
   joined the army.
   My older brother's **beard** is very thick, but my
   younger brother cannot grow a beard yet.

—beard

9. **ought to** [should]

> Members of a family **ought to** share the responsibilities of taking care of the house.
> We **ought to** move to a new house; this one is much too small.

10. **conversation** [talking with someone]

> My grandmother and I always have interesting **conversations** about what she did when she was young.
> **Conversations** with him are always so boring! He never has anything new to say.

11. **discussion** [a serious conversation]

> I hate having **discussions** about money at the dinner table.
> My parents often start to argue during **discussions** about my future.

12. **independent** [able to take care of oneself; able to do things without help; separate, alone]

> My sister was very **independent**. She got an apartment and a job at age seventeen and also paid for her university education.
> Her little girl wants to be **independent**. She does not want to hold on to her mother's hand on the street.

13. **angry** [feeling strong displeasure]

> My parents get **angry** if we use their belongings without asking first.
> My sister sometimes gets **angry** when she cannot do something she would like to.
> I am **angry** at him because he lied to me.

14. **although**

> **Although** she loves children, she does not have any of her own.
> **Although** she was angry, she smiled at her son.
> **Although** he ought to help us, he will not.
> His hair is blond **although** his parents' hair is dark.
> He grew a beard **although** he was only fifteen years old.

15. **adult** [a person who is fully grown]

> People over the age of eighteen are usually considered **adults**.
> Being older does not mean a person always behaves like an **adult**.

16. **approve** (of) [to think of something as appropriate or right]

> My parents **approve of** my decision to go to college.
> I do not **approve of** some of my sister's behavior.

17. **kiss** [to touch with the lips as a sign of love]

> My parents always **kissed** us goodnight before we went to bed.
> My brother and his wife **kissed** us when they arrived for a visit.
> We **kissed** them goodbye before they got on the plane.

18. **jealousy** [a feeling of wanting someone else's belongings or accomplishments because they are better than yours]

> My brothers, sisters, and I are never **jealous** of each other. We have had equal opportunities and support each others' accomplishments.
> My aunt was **jealous** when she heard that my mother got a new car.

19. **rely** (on) [to trust someone, knowing that he will do things when you ask or when he promises]

> My parents can **rely on** us to take care of the house while they are away.
> Our grandparents **rely on** us for money.

Introductory Exercises

A. Match each word with its definition.

_____ **1.** to permit
_____ **2.** should
_____ **3.** full of feeling
_____ **4.** strong displeasure
_____ **5.** a baby younger than one year old
_____ **6.** rely on
_____ **7.** a woman soon to be married
_____ **8.** to talk with someone
_____ **9.** not a child
_____ **10.** things that you own

a. adult
b. anger
c. belongings
d. bride
e. converse
f. depend on
g. emotional
h. infant
i. jealous
j. let
k. misbehave
l. ought to

B. Complete the following sentences.

1. If you have light hair, you are _____ .
2. If you are not a child, you are a(n) _____ .

3. If someone does something bad to you, you might get

_____ .

4. If you are impolite, that is bad _____ .
5. If you think well of something, you _____ of it.
6. Love, hate, anger, happiness are _____-s .
7. If he always does what he says, you can _____ on him.
8. If you behave badly, you are _____ .

Study Exercises

C. Use the definitions, descriptions, or examples to complete the blanks.

F A M I L Y

1. to accept as right	A __ __ __ __ __ __
2. feelings	__ M __ __ __ __ __ __
3. a sign of love or caring	__ I __ __
4. light hair	__ L __ __ __
5. to depend on	__ __ __ Y
6. a young baby	__ __ F __ __ __
7. facial hair	__ __ A __ __
8. to be bad in how you act	M __ __ __ __ __ __ __
9. a conversation	__ I __ __ __ __ __ __ __ __
10. to be part of	__ __ L __ __ __
11. feeling very strong displeasure	__ __ __ __ Y

D. Write **T** if the sentence is true and **F** if it is false.

——— **1.** Anger, jealousy, and love are emotions.

——— **2.** To have a good conversation, you must scream.

——— **3.** There are many blond people in Scandinavia.

——— **4.** An infant is old enough to begin school.

——— **5.** Children who scream and break into adults' conversations are misbehaving.

——— **6.** In many areas of the world, it is not polite to kiss in public.

——— **7.** Ten-year-old boys can grow beards.

——— **8.** A woman is called a bride only after her husband dies.

——— **9.** A person who does not finish his work, does not arrive on time, and does not pay his bills is unreliable.

——— **10.** Generally, if you disapprove of something, you do not like it.

E. Read the passage and answer the questions that follow.

When I was a child, I could not wait to become an adult.
I wanted very badly to be independent and to live alone so
that I did not have to do what my parents wanted me to do. I
could leave my dirty clothes on the floor if I wanted to or
5 leave the dirty dishes in the sink for a week if I so wished.

I did not want to have to rely on anybody. I wanted a job
so that I did not have to depend on my parents for money. I
could not wait to buy my own car so that I did not have to
depend on other people to take me places.

10 I also did not want to rely on anyone for a place to live. I
wanted my own apartment so that my parents could not
disapprove if I came home too late or had loud parties. Also,
with my own apartment, no one could get angry at me if I
shut the door too loudly, forgot to turn the lights off, or

15 stood with the refrigerator door open. If I lived alone, no
longer would there be long discussions about who I was
going out with, when I would return, where I was going, and
other typical questions my parents asked. Everything in the
apartment would be my own belongings, my things—life

20 would be excellent!

Or so I thought! Now that I am an adult, I look back and
laugh. I can see how infantile my thoughts about adulthood
really were. Independence is a very difficult situation, with a
lot of responsibilities and emotional stress. I sometimes want

25 to be a dependent child again.

1. What did this person want to become? _____

   _____

2. Did he want to stay dependent? _____

   _____

3. Why did he want a job and his own car? _____

   _____

4. What are his four reasons for wanting to have his own apartment?

   a. _____

   b. _____

   c. _____

   d. _____

5. Why does he look back at his thoughts and laugh? _____

   _____

6. What does he know now that he did not know as a child? _____

   _____

7. What does he sometimes want to be now? _____

   _____

F.   Read the passage and answer the questions that follow.

      When my brothers, sister, and I were little, we were a big
responsibility for my parents. We were very active children,
so my parents had to be alert at all times. We were not
always well-behaved and frequently did things my mother
5 disapproved of. We got dirty when playing outside and made
a lot of noise when playing inside. On occasion, we got into
arguments with the neighbors' children; I still remember
putting dirty water on a neighbor's blond hair because we
were arguing about something. I got into a lot of trouble for
10 that.
      Although our parents disapproved of many things that
we did, they usually did not get very angry. They always
tried to discuss the situation with us the first time and rarely
screamed at us. I remember having long conversations about
15 why we ought to behave in a certain way.

My brothers, sister, and I always laughed and joked with each other. I can still remember how we joked with our older brother when he first was able to grow a beard. He was very proud of his "beard," but we all laughed because it was
20 nothing more than three or four blond hairs on his face. My mother always looked at us disapprovingly when we laughed so loudly, but my brother never got angry. He thought it was funny.

My sister, however, did get very angry on several
25 occasions. We always let each other use our belongings, but we had to ask permission before taking them. One time, I borrowed my sister's white dress without asking and got juice on it. When she found out, she screamed at me angrily, telling me that I was unreliable and infantile. I felt very sad,
30 and my mother was unhappy because I broke our family's rule about borrowing belongings. It was a very emotional situation. My sister and I talked and talked, and finally I kissed her to show her that I was sorry.

1. What does this girl tell you about their childhood behavior? _____

_____

2. How did their mother frequently feel about her children's

behavior? _____

_____

3. What problem did these children occasionally have with other

children? _____

_____

4. What is an example of a bad thing this girl did during an

argument? _____

_____

5. Instead of getting angry, what did these parents do? _____

_____

6. What did the children joke about with their older brother? _____

_____

7. What did their mother do when they laughed at their older

   brother? _____

   _____

8. Why did the sister get angry? _____

   _____

9. What did the sister do and say when she got angry? _____

   _____

10. What kind of situation did the argument become? _____

    _____

11. How did she show her sister she was sorry? _____

    _____

Follow-up

G. Write the sentences that your teacher reads aloud.

1. _____
2. _____
3. _____
4. _____
5. _____

H. Answer **TRUE** or **FALSE**.

1. Children depend on their parents for food and clothing.
2. An infant is a young baby.
3. Japanese and Koreans have blond hair.
4. Births and deaths are emotional situations for people in the family.
5. Conversing with people from France is a good way to improve your ability to speak French.
6. Adults always behave in an infantile way.
7. Brides in the United States always wear black dresses.

8. Letting children stay up until 2:00 A.M. makes it difficult for them to get up in the morning.
9. Parents often get angry when their children misbehave in public.
10. Parents ought to teach their children good behavior.

I. Answer the following questions.

1. What is jealousy? What are some typical reasons why people get jealous?
2. What does it mean to be independent? What are some responsibilities of independence?
3. What does it mean to be an adult? Does "adult" refer to an age or a behavior?
4. When is it acceptable to show anger? With whom? Where?
5. How do your parents deal with poor behavior?
6. What can make you angry?
7. What is the usual color of a bride's wedding dress in your country? Is it the same color in all countries?
8. What are some reasons that people kiss?
9. What do you and your family commonly discuss at the dinner table?
10. What types of things do your parents disapprove of?
11. What types of things do or did your parents let you do although they disapproved of them?

Food

Word Form Chart

NOUN	VERB	ADJECTIVE	ADVERB
			afterward(s)
amount	amount		
appetite		appetizing	
beer			
bottle	bottle	bottled	
burn	burn	burned	
		burning	
butter	butter	buttered	
candy		candied	
closure	close	closed	
		closing	
container	contain	contained	
contents			
dish	dish		
dozen			
flavor	flavor	flavorful	
		flavored	
ham			
hold	hold (held, held)		
holder			
	keep (kept, kept)		
sharpness	sharpen	sharp	sharply
smell	smell	smelly	
taste	taste	tasty	
touch	touch		

Definitions and Examples

1. keep (a) [to store; to save for later use]

> We **keep** a lot of food in our refrigerator.
> He decided to **keep** the old knives.

(b) [to stay fresh or in good condition]

> Bread will **keep** if you store it in a cool, dry place.

2. container [anything used to keep other things in]

> He put the food in a glass **container**.
> What kind of **container** did you use to carry the water?
> The **container** broke when she let it fall.

3. dish [an open, shallow container used for food]

> My mother put a big plate of meat, a **dish** of corn, a **dish** of
> potatoes, and a bowl of salad on the table for dinner.
> I usually wash the **dishes** as soon as we finish eating because they
> are harder to wash after food has dried on them.

4. appetite [a physical need for food]

> She has a big **appetite** and always eats a lot.
> He did not have a good **appetite** because he was sick.

5. ham [the meat from the leg of a pig]

> He ate a **ham** sandwich for lunch.
> We bought a large **ham** for the party.

6. hold (a) [to contain]

> Our refrigerator is very small. It can only **hold** enough food for
> three days.
> Our dining room can **hold** fifteen people.

(b) [to make something stay in a certain position]

> I **held** the plate while my mother put the meat on it.

7. bottle [a container with a narrow opening that can be closed, for
holding liquids]

> The child took the water **bottle** from the refrigerator.
> We bought several **bottles** of Coca-Cola.
> All **bottles** used to be made of glass.

8. **dozen** [a group of twelve]

   We bought a **dozen** eggs when we went shopping.
   About a **dozen** guests were already at the party when we arrived.
   Bakeries sell many things by the **dozen**.

9. **sharp** [able to cut easily]

   The edge of the knife was very **sharp**.
   She cut her finger on something **sharp**.
   To make cooking easier, you should always keep your knives **sharp**.

10. **burn** [to cook until black; to damage something with heat or with fire]

    My brother was angry when he **burned** the ham.
    When she **burned** her finger, she held it under the cold water.
    The guests arrived two hours late, so the dinner was a little **burned**.

11. **amount** [how much or how many of something]

    The food bill was an unbelievable **amount** of money.
    That **amount** will not be enough to serve six people. You will have
       to cook more.

12. **close** [to shut]

    She forgot to **close** the bread bag, so the bread got dry.
    The container **closes** very tightly to keep food fresh.
    The oven door **closed** on her hand and burned her.

13. **touch** [to let one thing come into contact with another thing]

    When the cold water **touched** the hot dish, the dish broke.
    She got burned when she **touched** the stove.
    Do not **touch** the food unless you have clean hands.

14. **candy** [a food usually made of sugar]

    We bought a dozen pieces of **candy**.
    Children usually prefer **candy** to fruit, but **candy** is bad for their
       teeth.

15. **taste** [to place something in the mouth in order to know if the thing is
    salty, sweet, etc.]

    He **tasted** the meat to see if it was too salty.
    Children like the **taste** of candy.
    The dinner did not **taste** very good because we cooked it too fast.
    The wine had a very sweet **taste**.
    Does water have a **taste**?

16. **flavor** [how something tastes]

   We really did not like the **flavor** of the vegetables; they tasted old.

   A: What **flavor** of candy do you like?
   B: I prefer orange and lemon.

17. **afterward(s)** [after that]

   We ate dinner and **afterward** had coffee and cake.
   Mary washed the dishes; **afterwards**, she finished her homework.

18. **beer** [a drink]

   Many people drink **beer** while watching sporting events.
   Beer can make you get drunk and act strangely if you drink too
      much of it.
   We never drink **beer** with our meals; we only have wine.

19. **butter** [a yellow or white food made from milk, often eaten on bread or
   used for cooking]

   We cooked our eggs in **butter**.
   I put **butter** on my bread.
   Butter adds flavor to vegetables.

20. **smell**

   He **smelled** the meat to see if it was still fresh.
   We could **smell** the meat burning.
   The kitchen **smelled** of fish.

Introductory Exercises

A. Match each word with its definition.

___ 1. taste
___ 2. able to cut
___ 3. to contain
___ 4. a shallow container
___ 5. to cook too long
___ 6. meat from a pig
___ 7. how much
___ 8. a container for liquids
___ 9. twelve

a. amount
b. bottle
c. burn
d. container
e. dish
f. dozen
g. flavor
h. ham
i. hold
j. keep
k. sharp

B. Answer each question with words from the word form chart in this unit.

1. What is something you can put in a dish?
2. What is something you can put in a bottle?
3. What tastes sweet?
4. What do you use your nose for?
5. What do you do to know the flavor of something?
6. What is something you will not do if the stove is hot?
7. What word describes a food that looks very tasty?
8. What happens if a food is in the oven too long?
9. What kind of container is usually made of glass?

Study Exercises

C. Circle the word which is different in meaning.

1. hold   burn   keep   contain
2. beef   ham   bacon   pork
3. taste   touch   talk   smell
4. bottle   dish   knife   container

D. In the blanks, write the appropriate word(s) from the word form chart in this unit.

1. He cut his finger on a(n) _____ knife.
2. The ice cream _____-ed delicious.
3. They kept the iced tea in a glass _____ .
4. We had _____ and potatoes for dinner.
5. We put _____ and salt on the vegetables.
6. Plates, bowls, cups, and glasses are all _____-es .
7. To feel if something is soft, you must _____ it.
8. Eggs are usually sold by the _____ .
9. The kitchen _____-ed really bad after we burned the fish.

E. Read the passage and answer the questions that follow.

Restaurants require their cooks to handle food carefully
to be sure that it stays fresh and does not make people ill.

First of all, the cook must keep the kitchen clean so that no dust, dirt, or dirty water comes into contact with the food he
5 will serve. He must keep all food which can go bad in closed containers in the refrigerator. Uncooked meat, for example, should be frozen or kept in the refrigerator in a covered dish. Salad and other vegetables should be kept in a covered bowl so that they stay fresh. Milk, juices, and other drinks and
10 liquids should be kept in closed bottles and kept cool. The cook must also be very careful to check the contents of the refrigerator frequently and throw away any food that looks or smells bad. He must also be sure that the amount of food in the refrigerator is not too great for the refrigerator to keep
15 cool. If a cook is careful with the food before he prepares it, as well as when he cooks it, he can be sure that it will be flavorful when he serves it to his customers.

1. Why should the cook handle restaurant food with care? _____

_____

2. Why should he keep the kitchen clean? _____

_____

3. How should he keep food such as meat and salad? _____

_____

4. When should the cook throw food away? _____

_____

5. What will happen when the amount of food is too great for the

refrigerator to handle? _____

_____

F. Read the passage and answer the questions that follow.

There are many ways to keep your kitchen safe. First, be sure that your stove and refrigerator are clean and in good working condition. If you smell gas near your stove, for example, you will know that it is not working correctly and
5 that someone should repair it. You will also want to keep your stove free from dirt and oil so that fires cannot start in the kitchen. Keeping the inside of the refrigerator free from ice is a good idea so that all the contents stay as cool as possible. Keep all sharp knives in a knife holder so that no
10 one gets cut or has a serious accident. Wash all sharp knives

separately from the rest of the dishes; in other words, do not put sharp knives in the water with bowls, plates and other dishes. You may reach into the water, touch the sharp end of a knife and cut your hand. Keep all dishes and glass
15 containers stored carefully so that none falls and breaks. When cooking food, you should keep all the handles of the pots away from the edge of the stove. This will make sure that no one hits the handles when walking by and gets burned by a falling pot. Finally, you should be prepared for
20 fires, burns, or other accidents. Near the stove you can keep a bag of flour or other similar dry material which is perfect for stopping small kitchen fires. In the case of a burn, some people run cool water over the burn. Be sure to keep all necessary telephone numbers in an obvious place in case you
25 have a more serious kitchen accident.

Give some ideas based on the passage for safety in the kitchen:

1. (with the stove and refrigerator) _____

_____

_____

_____

2. (with knives and glass containers) _____

_____

_____

_____

3. (with cooking pots) _____

_____

_____

_____

4. (with kitchen accidents) _____

_____

_____

_____

Follow-up

G. Write the sentences that your teacher reads aloud.

1. _____

2. _____

3. _____

4. _____

5. _____

H. Answer **TRUE** or **FALSE**.

1. Ham and pork come from the same animal.
2. People eat butter as they eat candy.
3. Meat is kept in bottles.
4. Candy contains a lot of sugar.
5. The flavor of burned food is delicious.
6. Food should be kept in closed containers.
7. Sharp knives make it easier to cut meat.
8. Often your appetite decides the amount of food you eat.
9. Ten eggs is the same as a dozen eggs.
10. "Flavor" and "taste" have the same meaning.

I. Answer the following questions.

1. What kind of appetite do you have? What amount of food do you normally eat at meal time? Give an example of what you might have.
2. What are your two favorite flavors?
3. What food smells the best to you?
4. What smells make you think of your home?
5. How do you keep your food fresh?
6. What kind of candy do you like? What new kind of candy have you tasted recently?
7. What do you do when you burn yourself? When you cut yourself on a sharp knife?
8. Is beer popular in your country? What drinks are popular? What drinks are not popular?

Housing

Word Form Chart

NOUN	VERB	ADJECTIVE	ADVERB	PREPOSITION
attachment	attach	attached		
carpet	carpet	carpeted		
carpeting				
ceiling				
dampness	dampen	damp		
deposit	deposit	deposited		
due		due	duly	
dust	dust	dusty		
elevator	elevate	elevated		
gate				
	hang (hung, hung)	hanging		
interior		interior		
knock	knock			
	lay (laid, laid)			
				per
porch		porch		
rear		rear		
	ruin	ruined		
step	step			
vacancy	vacate	vacant		
welcome	welcome	welcome		
		unwelcome		
		welcoming		

Definitions and Examples

1. **vacant** [empty]

   > There are three **vacant** houses on our street.
   > The apartment building stood **vacant** for three years before the city finally tore it down.

2. **rear** [the back of something]

   > Parking is available in the **rear**.
   >
   > A: Do they have a yard?
   > B: Yes. It's at the **rear** of the house.

3. **damp** [a little wet]

   > Our basement is always **damp**.
   > It looks as if it rained; the sidewalks are all **damp**.

4. **hang** (on) (from) [to hold from above so that the lower part is free]

   > We **hung** two new pictures **on** our living room wall.
   > In many European cities flower baskets **hang from** all the street lights.

5. **elevator** [a vehicle that carries people from one floor to another]

   > Our apartment building has two **elevators**.
   > We have to use the stairs when the **elevators** are out of order.

6. **interior** [the inside]

   > The **interior** of that old house needs a lot of work.
   > The outside is in bad condition, but the **interior** is almost like new.

7. **dust** [a layer of dirt that collects on furniture, or dirt that blows in the wind]

   > She probably had not cleaned in several weeks; there was **dust** all over everything.
   > It was very hard to see with the wind blowing **dust** into our faces.

8. **deposit** [an amount of money paid (often to a landlord) which is returned later]

   > The landlord will keep our **deposit** if we break our contract.
   > A **deposit** is paid only one time and is usually equal to one month's rent.

9. **ceiling** [the part of a room that is above your head, opposite the floor]

   Our house is very old, so the **ceilings** are very high.
   We never use the lights that are on the **ceiling**; we use only the table lamps.

10. **ruin** [to damage very badly or completely]

    The rain **ruined** many yards in our neighborhood.
    They **ruined** the beauty of the house by painting it orange.

11. **carpet** [a soft material which covers the floor]

    The children ran across the white **carpet** with their dirty shoes.
    My mother brought back a beautiful oriental **carpet** from Beijing.
    We have wall-to-wall **carpets** in our house.

12. **gate** [the door in a fence]

    We forgot to close the **gate**, so the dog was able
       to leave the yard.
    They have a **gate** at the apartment parking lot
       to prevent outsiders from using the lot.

    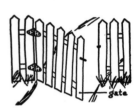

13. **attach** (to) [to put two things together]

    Our house has an **attached** two-car garage.
    The gate is **attached to** the fence.

14. **knock** [to make a sound on a door, table, etc., by hitting it]

    We **knocked** several times, but no one answered the door.
    You have to **knock** very loudly for the landlord to hear you.

15. **lay** [to put something down]

    We **laid** the deposit check on the desk.
    The men came to **lay** the carpeting in our living and dining rooms.

16. **porch** [a flat wooden or stone area outside the entrance of a house]

    We decided to have dinner outside on the
       porch instead of in the kitchen.
    The children play on the **porch** when it
       rains so that they do not get wet.
    We have some comfortable chairs on our
       porch so that we can sit there and relax.

17. **per** [for each; for every]

    Rent there is $300 **per** month. If we divide that amount among the
       three of us, it comes to $100 **per** person **per** month.

18. **due** (a) [expected at a certain time]

>Rent is **due** by the fifth of each month.
>Joe is **due** to arrive on the next flight.

    (b) [owed]

>I am **due** $50 because I paid too much deposit.
>The company is **due** a large amount from this customer.

19. **welcome** [admitted or received gladly somewhere]

>You are **welcome** to the house as often as you like.
>He always makes his guests feel **welcome**.

20. **step** (a) [each level of a set of stairs]

>Many people in the city sit on the front **step** in the evening.
>There are five **steps** leading to the front door.

    (b) [each move of one leg when you are walking or running]

>Watch your **step**! There is broken glass all over the porch.

Introductory Exercises

A. Match each word with its definition.

___ 1. empty	a. attach
___ 2. to put or take higher	b. carpet
___ 3. to damage badly	c. dampen
___ 4. the back of	d. dusty
___ 5. a floor covering	e. elevate
___ 6. to put down	f. gate
___ 7. a door in a fence	g. interior
___ 8. to make wet	h. lay
___ 9. the inside	i. rear
___ 10. to put together	j. ruin
	k. step
	l. vacant

B. Answer **TRUE** or **FALSE**.

1. You put carpets on the ceiling.
2. Basements are often damp.
3. A porch is on the outside of a house.
4. People welcome dust in their houses.

5. Floods can ruin houses and stores.
6. You commonly hang pictures on the ceiling.
7. When no one lives in a building, it is vacant.
8. Knocking on the door tells people that you would like to enter the room.
9. Dampness can ruin furniture.
10. Houses usually have gates in every room.

Study Exercises

C. Match each word with its opposite.

____	**1.** welcome	**a.** repair
____	**2.** dusty	**b.** separate
____	**3.** rear	**c.** outside
____	**4.** elevate	**d.** full
____	**5.** damp	**e.** floor
____	**6.** ruin	**f.** unwanted
____	**7.** attached	**g.** dry
____	**8.** interior	**h.** clean
____	**9.** ceiling	**i.** front
____	**10.** vacant	**j.** lower

D. In the blanks, write the appropriate word(s) from the word form chart in this unit.

1. You can ride the _____ to get to the fifth floor.
2. Be sure that you _____ before you enter the room so that you do not bother anybody.
3. Because we live near the ocean, the interior of our house is always _____ .
4. Rent is usually _____ at the beginning of the month.
5. _____ collects on everything if you do not clean often enough.
6. That apartment is more expensive because all the floors have _____ .
7. Our rent is $100 _____ month.
8. You are always _____ to stay with us when you visit our city.

E. Write the correct word in the blanks.

ACROSS

1. empty
3. expected at a certain time
5. a device to take people up or down
6. one part of a stairway
8. a soft floor covering
11. housing
12. the door in a fence
15. the inside
16. to make a noise on something with your hand

DOWN

2. put together
3. covered with a layer of dirt
4. to put in or on something
7. for each, for every
8. the part of the room above your head
9. to damage greatly
10. some wetness
13. the back part
14. the part of the house usually outside each entrance

F. Read the passage and answer the questions that follow.

Last week as my husband and I were driving near the beach, we noticed a small house with a For Rent sign. We went onto the front porch and knocked at the door, but no one answered, so we walked down the steps and around to
5   the rear of the house. There we found a small yard surrounded by a fence with an old metal gate.

Because the house was vacant, we decided to take a look inside. We looked in one of the windows near the back porch

and saw that the interior was dusty but in generally good
10 condition. The walls and floors were in perfect condition.
The only thing that needed repair was the ceiling in the
kitchen, which had been damaged, but not ruined, by some
rain water.

While we were looking, a neighbor came over to see who
15 we were. The house belonged to him, so he was able to take
us inside. There was a total of six rooms, and all but the
kitchen had carpeting. The house was unfurnished, but there
were still several pictures hanging in one of the rooms. In
general, the house looked wonderful.

20   The landlord explained to us that the rent was $350 per
month, due by the fifth day of each month, and that usually
he required a deposit equal to one month's rent. However, if
we would repair the ceiling, he would not charge us the
deposit. The idea sounded very good, so my husband and I
25 went home to discuss things. We decided to take it.

1. What did the couple do when they arrived on the front porch? _____

_____

2. Where did they go when no one answered the door? _____

_____

3. What did they find behind the house? _____

_____

4. Why did they think it was all right to look inside the house? _____

_____

5. What was wrong with the ceiling? _____

_____

6. How was the rest of the interior? _____

_____

7. Why did the neighbor come over? _____

_____

8. How much was the rent, and when was it due? _____

_____

9. What idea did the landlord have? _____

_____

Follow-up

G. Dictation: Write the sentences that your teacher reads aloud.

1. _____

2. _____

3. _____

4. _____

5. _____

H. Answer the following questions.

1. When can dust cause a problem for people?
2. Why should you knock before entering a room?
3. What does the interior of a typical house in your country look like?
4. What kinds of things do people in your country usually have on their walls and floors? In the living room? In the kitchen? etc.?
5. Do people commonly have porches in your country? What do people use them for?
6. What are some typical physical problems people might have with their apartments or houses?
7. Describe the rental/deposit system in your country.
8. Are you happy with your own housing situation? Why? Why not?

I. Describe the interior of your apartment or house.

Farming

Word Form Chart

NOUN	VERB	ADJECTIVE	ADVERB
bite	bite (bit, bitten)	bitten	
		biting	
cage	cage	caged	
calm	calm	calm	calmly
		calming	
		calmed	
dam	dam	dammed	
	dig (dug, dug)	digging	
		dug	
	double	double	
		doubled	
feather		feathery	
		feathered	
grain			
hunt	hunt	hunting	
		hunted	
hunting			
irrigation	irrigate	irrigated	
		immediate	immediately
provider	provide		
provision			
source			
tail			
village			
villager			
wild		wild	
wildness			
wilderness			

Definitions and Examples

1. **village** [a very small town]

    The farmers bring their vegetables to the **village** to sell them.
    They live in a **village** which has only five stores.

2. **calm** [very quiet, with no excitement]

    Life in the village is very **calm**.
    I am never **calm** before a test.

3. **feathers** [the things that cover a bird's body]

    The farmer took the **feathers** off the dead chicken.
    The lady wore a hat with some **feathers** on it.

    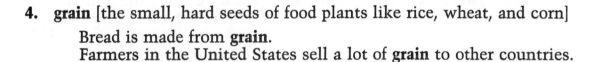

4. **grain** [the small, hard seeds of food plants like rice, wheat, and corn]

    Bread is made from **grain**.
    Farmers in the United States sell a lot of **grain** to other countries.

5. **provide** [to give, to make available]

    The farmers **provide** food for the people who live in the cities.
    The hotel **provided** us with breakfast.

6. **wild** [in nature; not accustomed to humans]

    Wild animals are sometimes dangerous.
    Some food plants grow in the **wild**, but most are grown by man.

7. **hunt** [to follow a wild animal to kill it, for food or for sport]

    Some people like to **hunt**, but others think it is a horrible sport.
    The government limits **hunting** to special areas.

8. **irrigation** [a system made by man for providing water for crops]

    That farmer does not have an **irrigation** system for his fields; if
    there is no rain, the crops will die.
    Irrigation is very important to farmers in dry areas.

9. **source** [the place from which something comes]

    The **source** of water for our irrigation system is the river near our
    farm.
    The farms in the country are the **source** of food for the cities.

10. **dam** [a wall which holds water in place]

> We need a **dam** to provide water for our irrigation system.
> When the **dam** broke, the town was flooded.

11. **double** [two times as much]

> The big farm is **double** the size of this smaller one.
> That farmer **doubled** the amount of crops he produces by using irrigation.

12. **bite** [to take a piece of something with the teeth]

> Some wild animals may **bite** you if you get close to them.
> The mailman screamed when the dog **bit** him.

13. **immediately** [now, without losing time]

> The animal ran away **immediately** when he heard the hunter.
> If you see a fire, you should call the firemen **immediately**.

14. **cage** [a place to keep an animal so that it does not run away]

> The dangerous animals at the zoo are in **cages**.
> When I take my cat in the car, I put him in a small **cage**.

15. **dig** [to make a hole in the ground]

> The dog ran away by **digging** a hole under the fence.
> The farmer **dug** small holes to put the seeds in.

16. **tail** [the long part of the body at the back of many kinds of animals]

> Humans do not have **tails**.
> Most dogs and cats have **tails**.
> Only the **tail** of the cat was moving.

Introductory Exercises

A.   Match each word with its definition.

_____ 1. to give, to make available	**a.** bite
_____ 2. two times as much	**b.** cage
_____ 3. the place from which something comes	**c.** calm
	d. dam
_____ 4. to follow a wild animal to kill it	**e.** dig
	f. double
_____ 5. a place to keep an animal	**g.** feathers
_____ 6. the small, hard seeds of some food plants	**h.** grain
	i. hunt
_____ 7. in nature, not accustomed to humans	**j.** irrigation
	k. immediately
_____ 8. a system made by man for providing water for crops	**l.** provide
	m. source
_____ 9. very soon after something	**n.** tail
_____ 10. the things that cover a bird's body	**o.** village
	p. wild
_____ 11. a very small town	
_____ 12. very quiet, with no excitement	

B.   Answer each question with a word from the word form chart in this unit.

1. What are you doing when you make a hole in the ground?
2. What kind of animals live in the forest?
3. What might an angry dog do to you?
4. If something will happen very, very soon, when will it happen?
5. What do birds have on their bodies?
6. What do some people use guns for?
7. What do most dogs and cats have that humans do not have?
8. If a town is very small, what is it?
9. What are rice and wheat?
10. What do farmers do to their fields when it does not rain?
11. What do the animals at the zoo live in?
12. How can you describe life in a small village?
13. What is a place where something starts or comes from?

Study Exercises

C. Write **T** if the sentence is true and **F** if it is false.

_____ **1.** Wet places need irrigation.

_____ **2.** Life in a big city is usually calm.

_____ **3.** You can find cages at most zoos.

_____ **4.** Parents provide food and love for their children.

_____ **5.** Wild animals may bite.

_____ **6.** If you double ten, you get twenty.

_____ **7.** Cats have feathers.

_____ **8.** A desert is a good source of water.

_____ **9.** If you must do something immediately, you should hurry to do it.

_____ **10.** Dams hold water.

_____ **11.** Hunting hurts animals.

_____ **12.** People eat grains.

D. Circle the word which is different in meaning.

1. calm   quiet   double

2. feather   provision   fur

3. village   city   source

4. dig   immediately   soon

5. food   dam   grain

6. cage   head   tail

7. irrigate   hunt   search

E. Read the passage and answer the questions that follow.

    The local farmers came to the village of Westview yesterday to discuss their need for a new dam. They met with agriculture specialists from the central government. The farmers' complaint is that the Blue River, which is the source
5 of the water they use to irrigate their fields, almost disappears each summer. The old dam, which was dug more than 40 years ago, does not hold enough water to provide all of the farmers with the water they need. The farmers estimate that they need more than double the amount of
10 water that is currently available.

The meeting was noisy at times, with the farmers arguing for immediate action by the government. However, the government specialists calmed the farmers by promising to complete the new dam by the beginning of the next
15 planting season.

1. What is Westview? _____

_____

2. Why is the Blue River important to the farmers? _____

_____

3. When was the old dam built? _____

_____

4. What is the problem with the old dam? _____

_____

5. How much more water do the farmers need? _____

_____

6. What do the farmers want from the government? When? _____

_____

7. How did the specialists calm the farmers? _____

_____

Follow-up

F.   Dictation: Write the sentences that your teacher reads aloud.

    1. _____

    2. _____

    3. _____

    4. _____

    5. _____

G. Answer the following questions.

1. Have you visited a wilderness area of your country? Where? What was it like?
2. What animals do people in your country hunt?
3. Are there any dangerous wild animals in your country? Which ones?
4. Have you been bitten by an animal? By a wild animal? What happened?
5. Name some things that feathers can be used to make.
6. Have you lived in a village? Describe the life there.
7. Do the farmers in your country use irrigation? What is the source of the water?
8. Which grains are commonly eaten in your country? What is the source of these grains?
9. What do you do to stay calm before important tests?

H. Complete the story.

Mr. Brown owns a farm. It is summer now, and the weather has been very dry. . . .

Government

Word Form Chart

NOUN	VERB	ADJECTIVE	ADVERB
agreement	agree	agreeable	agreeably
disagreement	disagree	disagreeable	disagreeably
apology	apologize	apologetic	apologetically
consideration	consider	considered	
doubt	doubt	doubtful	doubtfully
			undoubtedly
import	import	imported	
importation			
majority			
minority			
opposition	oppose	opposite	
		opposing	
opponent		opposed	
party			
politics		political	politically
politician			
population	populate	populated	
poverty			
representative	represent	representative	representatively
representation		represented	
tax	tax	taxed	

Definitions and Examples

1. **population** [the number of people who live in a place]

    The **population** of the United States is about two hundred million.

    A: What is the **population** of your city?
    B: About 500,000.

2. **tax** [the money which the people in a country must pay to the government]

    The government is not popular now because **taxes** are high.
    The president promised not to increase **taxes**.

3. **apologize** (for) [to say that you are sorry about something]

    The president **apologized** to the people for increasing their taxes.
    The people accepted his **apology** because they knew that the government needed the money.

4. **agree** (with) [to say "yes" to someone's idea; to have the same opinion as someone else]

    Most of the population **agrees** with the president's plan.
    The two countries **agreed** to stop fighting; this **agreement** should end the war.

5. **politics** [the science of government]

    Many members of the Kennedy family have entered American **politics**.
    The **politician** did not want to answer the media's questions.
    The **political** situation in that country is always changing; they have had six presidents in the last two years.

6. **poverty** [the condition of being poor]

    The government does not want the amount of **poverty** in the country to increase.
    Poor people live in **poverty**.
    Children who are raised in **poverty** often have trouble in school.

7. **represent** [to act or speak for other people]

    We elect people to **represent** us in the government.
    A **representative** should pay attention to the opinions of the people he **represents**.

8. **party** [a group of people with similar political opinions who try to get people elected]

> The U.S. has two major political **parties**.
> The **party** which wins the election will have a lot of power for the next two years.

9. **doubt** [to feel unsure about something]

> I **doubt** that his party can win the election; they are not very popular.
> Taxes will **undoubtedly** rise soon because the government needs the money.

10. **majority** [the larger part of a number; more than half]

> He won the election because the **majority** of the people voted for him.
> In a democracy, the **majority** rules.

11. **minority** [the smaller part of a number; less than half]

> Black people are a **minority** group in the United States.
> Only a **minority** of the people voted for him, so he lost the election.

12. **import** [to bring things into a country]

> The U.S. **imports** a lot of cars from Japan.
> The government taxes **imports**.

13. **consider** [to think about; to have an opinion]

> The government is **considering** raising taxes on imported cars and should make a decision soon.
> Most people **consider** him to be a good president.
> The new plan is under **consideration**.

14. **oppose** [to be against]

> Two people **opposed** her in the election, but she won a clear majority of the votes.
> The **opposition** party does not have enough power to win this election.
> The people with the **opposite** opinion argued strongly against us.

Introductory Exercises

A. Match each word with its definition.

_____ 1. the science of government

_____ 2. the people who live in a place

_____ 3. to be against

_____ 4. more than half

_____ 5. to bring things into a country

_____ 6. to feel unsure about something

_____ 7. to act or speak for other people

_____ 8. to say that you are sorry

_____ 9. to have the same opinion as someone else

_____ 10. the condition of being poor

_____ 11. the money that the people in a country must pay to the government

_____ 12. less than half

a. agree
b. apologize
c. consider
d. doubt
e. import
f. majority
g. minority
h. oppose
i. party
j. politics
k. population
l. poverty
m. represent
n. tax

B. Complete each sentence with a word from the word form chart in this unit.

1. Becoming the president of a country means entering

   _____ .

2. That country does not grow any grains, so they have to be

   _____ -ed .

3. In order to restrict imports, the two countries signed an

   _____ .

4. They do not have enough to eat; they are living in

   _____ .

5. People do not like to pay _____ .

6. He will win the election for sure because he has no

   _____ .

7. Although he was angry with his opponent, he accepted the

   _____ .

8. That country is a democracy and has three major political

   _____ .

Study Exercises

C.   Write **T** if the sentence is true and **F** if it is false.

_____ 1. Most people like to pay taxes.

_____ 2. A governing party does not usually agree with its opposition.

_____ 3. Cities have higher populations than villages.

_____ 4. Taxes often make imported things expensive.

_____ 5. Rich people live in poverty.

_____ 6. The minority always agrees with the majority.

_____ 7. In democracies people vote for people to represent them in the government.

_____ 8. The opposition party is the party currently in power.

_____ 9. People apologize for good things they have done.

_____ 10. People sometimes doubt the word of politicians.

D.   Match each word with its opposite.

_____ 1. agree

_____ 2. consider

_____ 3. doubt

_____ 4. import

_____ 5. majority

_____ 6. oppose

_____ 7. populated

_____ 8. undoubtedly

a. not think about
b. agree with
c. political
d. disagree
e. misrepresent
f. not certainly
g. believe
h. without people
i. tax
j. minority
k. send out of the country

E.   Read the passage and answer the questions that follow.

> Yesterday a majority of representatives in the House of Representatives voted to increase taxes on imports of automobiles. The new law ends last year's informal agreement to permit unlimited imports. The new import tax
> 5 had been under consideration for several weeks before its approval yesterday.
>   The opposition party voiced its disapproval of the new import tax, saying that it was doubtful that the vote really represented the true opinions of the majority of the
> 10 population. The opposition doubts that the import tax will produce more jobs within the country, and so it feels that, as an effort to fight poverty, the new law will fail. A spokesman for the opposition said yesterday that the new law is only a result of political games and will hurt the country.

1. How many of the representatives voted for the new tax? _____

_____

2. On what basis were unlimited imports permitted until yesterday? __

_____

3. What long had the House of Representatives been considering the

new law? _____

_____

4. How does the opposition think that most people feel about the law?

_____

_____

5. What does the opposition think about the ability of the new law in

helping against poverty? Why? _____

_____

6. How does the opposition think that the new law was passed? _____

_____

Follow-up

F.   Dictation: Write the sentences that your teacher reads aloud.

1. _____

2. _____

3. _____

4. _____

5. _____

G.   Answer the following questions.

1. What types of things are imported into your country? How high are the prices of these things?
2. Which cities in your country have the highest populations?
3. Which areas of your country are not very populated?
4. Do you have to pay a tax on things that you buy in your country? How much?
5. Do you have to pay a tax on your earnings in your country? How much?
6. Do any areas of your country have much poverty? Which ones?
7. What do people in your country think of politicians? Is politics considered to be an honorable job? Why?

H.   Explain about:

1. The political system in your country.
2. The minority populations in your country.

Health

Word Form Chart

NOUN	VERB	ADJECTIVE	ADVERB
		alive	
ankle			
	bear (bore, born)	born	
birth			
brain			
chest			
deafness	deafen	deaf	
		deafening	
glasses			
heart			
knee			
neck			
normality	normalize	normal	normally
abnormality		abnormal	abnormally
recentness		recent	recently
	seem		seemingly
skin			
thermometer			
twist	twist	twisted	
		twisting	

Definitions and Examples

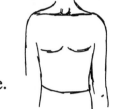

1. **neck** [the part of the body that holds the head up]

   A man may wear a tie around his **neck**.
   The small child put his arms tightly around his mother's **neck**.

2. **chest** [the top front part of the body, above the stomach and below the neck]

   The doctor examined the soldier's **chest**.
   A **chest** x-ray is sometimes necessary to find a disease.

3. **ankle** [the part of the body between the leg and the foot]

   I hurt my **ankle** playing soccer.
   This is a shallow river. The water comes only to
      my **ankle**.

4. **birth** [the beginning of a person's or an animal's life]

   We learned that the queen gave **birth** to a son.
   The **birth** of twins was not expected.

5. **brain** [the part of the body, located in the head, that allows us to act, learn, think, remember, etc.]

   The **brain** is protected by a strong bone.
   The human **brain** is very complicated.

6. **glasses** [the things worn in front of the eyes, to help you see better]

   I can see more things now because I have new **glasses**.

7. **heart** [the part of the body that moves the blood]

   Heart disease can result in death.
   What is causing this pain in my **heart**?

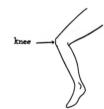

8. **knee** [the middle part of the leg, where it moves]

   She broke her **knee** in a serious fall.
   His boots come as high as his **knees**.

9. **twist** [to turn something around, to change the usual shape of something]

   If you **twist** your back, you might feel pain.
   Is you ankle broken or just **twisted**?

10. normal [usual; regular]

> **Normal** body temperature is 98.6 degrees Fahrenheit.
> It is **abnormal** to have a fever.

11. recently [not a long time ago]

> Have you checked the weather **recently**?
> I enjoyed my **recent** journey to Japan.

12. seem [to appear to be]

> This coin **seems** genuine.
> The storm **seems** to be coming closer.

13. deaf [not able to hear]

> It is difficult to communicate with my grandmother because she is
>   **deaf**.
> An injury to the ear can cause **deafness**.

14. skin [the outside covering of the body]

> The **skin** of animals is often used for clothing.
> A baby's **skin** is smooth.

15. thermometer [an instrument for measuring temperature]

> Maybe I have a fever. Where is the **thermometer**?
> The **thermometer** reads 82 degrees Fahrenheit.

16. alive [not dead; living]

> Only one person was found **alive** after the car accident.
> The soldier was happy to be **alive** after the war.

Introductory Exercises

A. Match each word with its definition.

____ **1.** the part of the body that moves the blood	**a.** alive
____ **2.** not long ago	**b.** ankle
____ **3.** the beginning of a life	**c.** birth
____ **4.** regular	**d.** brain
____ **5.** not able to hear	**e.** deaf
____ **6.** living	**f.** heart
____ **7.** to appear to be	**g.** normal
	h. recently
	i. seem

B. Answer each question with a word from the word form chart in this unit.

1. What part of your body helps you think?
2. What covers the outside of your body?
3. What instrument measures temperature?
4. What part of your body holds up your head?
5. What helps you to see better?
6. What part of your body is in the middle of your leg?
7. What part of your body contains your heart?

Study Exercises

C. In the blanks, write the appropriate word(s) from the word form chart.

1. The year of my _____ is a famous year in recent history.
2. Scientists know that the _____ has two hemispheres.
3. When the doctor examined my ankle, he said that it was just _____ -ed , not broken.
4. The size of your sweater depends on the measurement of your _____ .
5. This much rainfall is _____ for July.
6. The music _____ -s to be getting louder.
7. A nurse usually carries a(n) _____ .

D. Write **T** if the sentence is true and **F** if it is false.

_____ 1. Leather is really animal skin.
_____ 2. A twisted ankle is a painful injury.
_____ 3. The wheel was invented recently.
_____ 4. Complex language seems to be limited to humans.
_____ 5. Glasses help deaf people.
_____ 6. If you cannot breathe, you cannot stay alive.
_____ 7. You wear shoes on your neck.
_____ 8. Your heart rate increases during exercise.
_____ 9. A baby may weigh thirty pounds at birth.

E.   Write the correct word in the blanks.

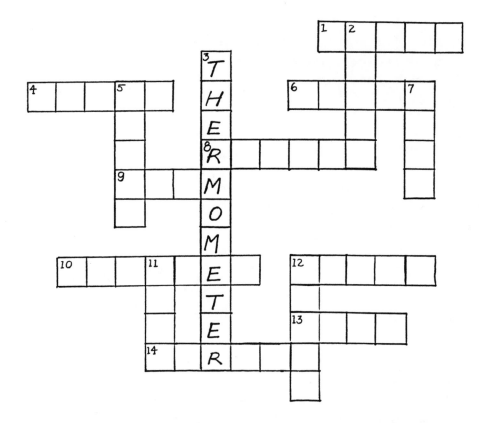

<table>
<tr><td colspan="3" align="center">ACROSS</td></tr>
</table>

ACROSS

1. the part of the body above the stomach and below the neck
4. the beginning of a life
6. it allows us to think and learn
8. not long ago
9. to appear to be
10. they help you to see better
12. living
13. part of the leg
14. usual ·

DOWN

2. it pumps the blood
3. it measures temperature
5. to change the usual shape
7. it holds the head up
11. it covers the body
12. part of the body between the leg and foot

F.   Read the passage and answer the questions that follow.

   Dr. Baskin recently graduated from medical school. He does not have a private office now, but he works instead in the emergency room of a big city hospital. Every day he sees many different diseases and injuries.

5   On Monday Dr. Baskin saw a woman who had given birth to a baby in a taxi. Dr. Baskin examined the baby and said that it was normal. On Tuesday he saw a man with a

serious heart abnormality. On Wednesday Dr. Baskin saw
two young men who had been in an automobile accident.
10 One had a broken knee and the other had a neck injury. On
Thursday he examined a baseball player who had twisted his
ankle, and on Friday he saw a very old woman who
complained of pains in her chest.
Dr. Baskin seems very happy with his new job because it
15 is so interesting.

1. Where does Dr. Baskin work? _____

_____

2. Where was the baby born on Monday? _____

_____

3. What problem did he see on Tuesday? _____

_____

4. What injuries did the two young men have? _____

_____

5. Who had a twisted ankle? _____

_____

6. What did the old woman complain about? _____

_____

7. Does Dr. Baskin like his job? _____

_____

Follow-up

G. Dictation: Write the sentences that your teacher reads aloud.

1. _____

2. _____

3. _____

4. _____

5. _____

H. Answer the following questions.

1. Have you ever twisted your neck, ankle, or knee? When? How?
2. Is heart disease a big problem in your country? Why or why not?
3. Have you had a chest X-ray recently? Why or why not?
4. What is the city of your birth?
5. Are your grandparents still alive?
6. Are there special schools for deaf children in your country?
7. Is the birth rate increasing or decreasing in your country? Why?
8. Do you know your birth weight? What was it?

I. Finish the story.

The ambulance driver was the first person to arrive at the intersection where the car had hit the bus.

Military

Word Form Chart

NOUN	VERB	ADJECTIVE	ADVERB
adventure		adventurous	adventurously
adventurer			
battle	battle		
bravery	brave	brave	bravely
captain	captain		
capture	capture	captured	
citizen			
citizenry			
crew	crew		
duty		dutiful	dutifully
explosion	explode	explosive	explosively
explosive		exploded	
		exploding	
invader	invade	invaded	
		invading	
invasion			
joint	join	joint	jointly
		joined	
nation		national	nationally
nationality			
nationalism			
scarcity		scarce	scarcely
selection	select	selective	selectively
		selected	
service	serve		
uniform		uniform	uniformly
		uniformed	
volunteer	volunteer	voluntary	voluntarily
weapon			
weaponry			

Definitions and Examples

1. **captain** (a) [a leader of a military group, ship, or airplane]

    The **captain** led his men into battle.
    My father was a **captain** in the army.

    (b) [the leader of a sports team]

    The **captain** told his team members to keep trying.

2. **adventure** [an experience that is exciting, unusual, dangerous, and difficult]

    My grandfather told us about his **adventures** as a sailor.
    The **adventurous** campers walked many miles into the forest.

3. **battle** [a big fight]

    The **battle** between the military airplanes lasted many days.
    The armies **battled** for control of the airport.

4. **brave** [showing no fear]

    The **brave** fireman carried the baby from the burning building.
    Bravery is an important characteristic for a soldier.

5. **citizen** [a person who lives in a country or town and is protected by its government]

    Some of the **citizens** of the small village were unhappy about the recent election.
    A majority of the **citizens** voted for the new president.

6. **crew** [the people who run a ship or an airplane]

    Sailors form the **crew** of a military ship.
    The **crew** of the airplane had difficulty flying in bad weather.

7. **duty** [something that a person should or must do]

    It is the **duty** of a citizen to pay his taxes.
    What **duties** does a child have toward his parents?

8. **capture** [to take and hold by force]

    If we do not **capture** the bridge, we will not win the war.
    It might be easier to **capture** the railroad station at night.

9. **explode** [to burst quickly and with a loud noise]

    The bomb **exploded** in the center of the city.
    Did you hear the **explosion** in the chemistry class?

10. **join** [to come together or put together; to become a member of]

    Would you like to **join** our basketball team?
    The knee and the ankle are **joints**.

11. **nation** [a country]

    Neighboring **nations** sometimes discuss important laws.
    Do you have parades on your **national** holiday?
    Your **nationality** is written on your official papers.

12. **scarce** [hard to get or find]

    Fresh fruit is **scarce** in winter.
    There is a **scarcity** of engineers in some poor countries.

13. **select** [to choose from several]

    Why did you **select** the red sweater but not the blue one?
    The **selection** of a leader is a complicated process.

14. **voluntary** (a) [not compulsory]

    Military service is **voluntary** in the United States now.

    (b) [by free choice]

    I sometimes **volunteer** to help my mother wash the dishes.

    (c) [done without pay]

    My mother does **volunteer** work at a hospital each week.

15. **serve** [to work under someone or something; to help, in a voluntary or compulsory way]

    My father **served** five years in the military.
    Military **service** is required for both men and women.

16. **invade** [to enter with force]

    The planes **invaded** the enemy air space.
    An **invasion** is sometimes easier by night.

17. **uniform** (a) [special clothes worn by the members of a group]

    He felt proud when he wore his air force **uniform**.
    A baseball player's **uniform** gets dirty during every game.

    (b) [always the same, not different from the others]

    Please use envelopes of **uniform** size.

18. **weapon** [an instrument used for fighting]

    A gun is a dangerous **weapon**.
    Have the police found the murder **weapon** yet?

Introductory Exercises

A. Match each word with its definition.

_____ 1. a country
_____ 2. to take by force and hold
_____ 3. showing no fear
_____ 4. a fight
_____ 5. an exciting experience
_____ 6. hard to find
_____ 7. to choose
_____ 8. to enter by force
_____ 9. to work for or to help
_____ 10. done without compulsion
_____ 11. something you should do

a. adventure
b. battle
c. brave
d. capture
e. crew
f. duty
g. invade
h. nation
i. scarce
j. select
k. serve
l. voluntary
m. weapon

B. Answer each question with a word from the word form chart in this unit.

1. Who lives in a country and is protected by that government?
2. Which people run a ship or an airplane?
3. What do you call something you should or must do?
4. What is a general name for knee or ankle?
5. What kind of clothes does a soldier or sailor wear?
6. What can be used to kill people?
7. Who is the leader of a group?
8. What does a bomb do?
9. Who likes exciting experiences?
10. What is another word for "choose"?

Study Exercises

C. Write **T** if the sentence is true and **F** if it is false.

_____ 1. Every sailor is a captain.
_____ 2. Citizens have a duty to break the law.
_____ 3. You should carry explosives with you in an airplane in your luggage.

_____ **4.** Each nation has only one language.

_____ **5.** You should be healthy to join the army.

_____ **6.** A strong military has modern weapons.

_____ **7.** An adventurer likes to stay at home.

_____ **8.** In history class we often learn the dates of famous battles.

_____ **9.** Soldiers and sailors wear uniforms.

_____ **10.** Fingers have several joints.

D. Circle the word which is different in meaning.

1. burst	explode	invade
2. country	village	nation
3. offer	choose	select
4. uniform	opposite	same
5. level	adventure	experience
6. battle	fight	obvious
7. leader	sand	captain
8. take	proceed	capture

E. In the blanks, write the appropriate word(s) from the word form chart in this unit.

1. A(n) _____ soldier is not afraid of fighting.

2. It is difficult for an army to _____ my country because of the high mountains.

3. Many products are _____ during times of war.

4. The ship's _____ had been at sea for many months and were happy to return home.

5. The _____ commanded his men to go into battle.

6. The clerk showed me a(n) _____ of her best shoes.

7. The _____ of my country vote often for government officials.

8. Military _____ is compulsory in many countries.

F.   Read the passage and answer the questions that follow.

> Miriam's favorite adventure movie is about an army captain in World War II. The movie begins when the young man volunteers for the military service and is selected for duty in Europe. He takes part in the invasion of France,
> 5 where he is injured as the result of an explosion.
> Miriam slept through part of the middle of the movie, but her friend described the battles and the capture of the nation's capital. However, Miriam remembers the conclusion very clearly. The final scene shows the brave captain as he
> 10 joins the other citizens for a parade and a party in the streets. She thinks he looks very handsome in his army uniform, and she wishes she had not fallen asleep.

1. What is Miriam's favorite movie about? _____

_____

2. Which country does the captain serve in? _____

_____

3. How is the captain injured? _____

_____

4. Why doesn't Miriam remember the middle of the movie? _____

_____

5. What does Miriam's friend describe? _____

_____

6. What does the captain do in the final scene? _____

_____

7. What makes the captain look handsome? _____

_____

Follow-up

G. Dictation: Write the sentences that your teacher reads aloud.

1. _____

2. _____

3. _____

4. _____

5. _____

H. Answer the following questions.

1. What is your nationality?
2. Do you do any work as a volunteer? What do you do?
3. Does your country spend a lot of money on weapons?
4. What colors are the police uniforms in your country?
5. What products are scarce in your country?
6. What are the duties of a good citizen?
7. Do many people choose to join the military service in your country?
8. What is the date of a famous battle in history?

I. Describe an adventure using this situation. What will happen?

On your way downstairs to class, you see something under the stairs that looks like a bomb. You move closer to get a better look.

Sports

Word Form Chart

NOUN	VERB	ADJECTIVE	ADVERB
admiration	admire	admirable	admirably
		admiring	admiringly
amateur		amateurish	amateurishly
bar			
bet	bet (bet, bet)	betting	
catcher	catch (caught, caught)		
catch			
champion		champion	
championship			
delay	delay	delayed	
		delaying	
disappointment	disappoint	disappointing	disappointingly
		disappointed	disappointedly
enthusiasm		enthusiastic	enthusiastically
entirety		entire	entirely
		mad	madly
match	match	matched	
modesty		modest	modestly
oxygen			
pass	pass		
pole			
profession		professional	professionally
professional			

Definitions and Examples

1. **admire** [to think well of and to have respect for someone or something]

    We **admired** the skill of the two tennis players.

    The boy's **admiration** for his older brother was obvious; he wanted to do everything his brother did.

    A: Which American president did you **admire** most?
    B: John Kennedy.

2. **professional** [a person who does something, such as sports or theater, for pay]

    Professional baseball players sometimes earn more than $1,000,000 per year in the United States.

    Some American college football players become **professionals** when they graduate from college.

3. **bar** [a long, thin piece of metal or wood used in sports to jump over or to hang from]

    Bars are very popular on playgrounds; children like to hang from them and play on them.

    In some kinds of races runners must jump over **bars**.

4. **delay** [to cause to be late]

    The rain **delayed** the baseball game an hour.

    Our vacation was **delayed** two weeks because I broke my foot.

5. **bet** (on) [an agreement between people that a person who chooses the winner of a race or match will win money]

    When you **bet** on a horse at a horse race, you hope the horse wins. If it does, you may win a lot of money.

    I won $20 last fall because I **bet** that the Pittsburgh football team would win.

    A: Did you **bet** on the winner of the World Cup Soccer game?
    B: No. I never place **bets** on sports.

6. **catch** [to take hold of something that is moving]

    When you throw a ball to someone, he must **catch** it.

    The boys in my neighborhood practice throwing and **catching** a football.

    We went fishing on Saturday, and I **caught** five fish.

7. **champion** [the first place winner in a contest or match; something or someone that is very skilled in a field]

> The **champion** of today's tennis game will win $1,000.
> Mr. Jones has a **champion** horse; it has won more than fifteen races in the last year.
>
> A: Who won the international soccer **championship** in 1982?
> B: Italy.

8. **disappointment** [the feeling of sadness because a hope or expectation was not satisfied]

> The little boy's **disappointment** was great because he had to miss his school's trip to the museum.
> The cancellation of the baseball game **disappointed** the fans.

9. **amateur** [a person who does something, such as sports or theater, for pleasure, not for pay]

> **Amateurs** play sports because they like to play, not because they want to make a lot of money.
> When I was in college, I played on an **amateur** basketball team.

10. **mad** [angry]

> The students were **mad** because the teacher gave them a surprise test.
> Mr. and Mrs. Smith were **mad** at their son when he came home at 3:00 A.M.

11. **entire** [complete; all of something]

> It rained all day yesterday, and the **entire** football game was played in the rain.
> Everyone in the **entire** audience was sleeping by the end of the president's speech.

12. **match** [a game or contest between two teams or two people]

> The tennis **match** was very exciting to watch; it was impossible to say who was going to win until the end.
>
> A: Did you see the soccer **match** on TV?
> B: Yes. It was a disappointing game.
> A: Why?
> B: Because my favorite team lost!

13. **modest** [not having an opinion of yourself that is too high]

   The tennis player was not very **modest** about his tennis ability. He
      said that he could play anyone in the world and win.

   A: Did you know that Anne can speak seven languages?
   B: No. I didn't. She never said anything about that.
   A: I know. She's a very **modest** person and never says anything
      about her abilities.

14. **oxygen** [a chemical that is a gas in the air; its chemical symbol is "O"]

   People and animals need to breathe **oxygen** in order to live.
   There is less **oxygen** at high altitudes than at low altitudes.

15. **pass** (a) [to move or throw from one person to another]

   The football player unsuccessfully **passed** the football to another
      player on his team—the **pass** was incomplete.
   Passing is a very important skill in American football.

   (b) [not to fail]

   She easily **passed** all her courses this year.

16. **pole** [a long, thin piece of wood or metal]

   You can catch fish with a fishing **pole**; fishing **poles** used to be
      made of wood, but today they are often made of plastic.
   In some sports you use a long **pole** to help you jump over a
      high bar.

17. **realize** [to come to understand]

   Jim **realized** he had lost his wallet when he felt his empty pocket.
   The foreign students were sad when they **realized** they would not
      see their friend again.

18. **enthusiasm** [a very strong interest, admiration, or excitement]

   The professor's **enthusiasm** for her subject made her classes very
      enjoyable for the students.
   The tourists were very **enthusiastic** about their visit to Niagara
      Falls. They thought the view was beautiful.

Introductory Exercises

A.   Match each word with its definition.

_____ **1.** a person who does something for money

_____ **2.** all, complete

_____ **3.** to come to understand

_____ **4.** to think well of someone

_____ **5.** a contest

_____ **6.** a piece of metal to hang from

_____ **7.** to take hold of something that is moving

_____ **8.** the winner of a contest

_____ **9.** angry

_____ **10.** a person who does something for pleasure

_____ **11.** to make later

_____ **12.** strong interest or excitement

_____ **13.** to move something from one person to another

_____ **14.** not having too high an opinion of yourself

a. admire
b. amateur
c. bar
d. bet
e. catch
f. champion
g. delay
h. disappoint
i. enthusiasm
j. entire
k. mad
l. match
m. modest
n. pass
o. professional
p. pole
q. realize

B.   Answer each question with a word from the word form chart in this unit.

1. How do you feel if you fail a test?
2. What do we breathe from the air?
3. What do soccer players do with a ball?
4. When a baseball player hits a ball, what does the other team try to do?
5. What feeling do you have for a person you respect?
6. How did the Argentinian fans act when Argentina won the soccer championship in 1986?
7. If you hope to win money without working, what can you do?
8. What can you use to catch fish?
9. What kind of sports players compete in the Olympics?
10. What is a tennis player who gets money for playing?
11. What do most sports teams want to be?

Study Exercises

C. Write **T** if the sentence is true and **F** if it is false.

_____ 1. Students are usually enthusiastic when they get too much homework.
_____ 2. A modest person always talks about himself.
_____ 3. A match is disappointing for fans when their team loses.
_____ 4. Football players kick a bar to each other.
_____ 5. You shouldn't eat an entire ham at one time.
_____ 6. Parents get mad when their children don't tell the truth.
_____ 7. Amateur tennis players earn a lot of money.
_____ 8. Bad weather may delay an airplane flight.
_____ 9. A professional swimming team must have a good pole.
_____ 10. Champions frequently lose.
_____ 11. We don't need oxygen to live.
_____ 12. In soccer, when one player passes the ball, another player catches it with his hands.

D. Match each word or phrase with its synonym.

_____ 1. winner
_____ 2. angry
_____ 3. complete
_____ 4. contest
_____ 5. strong interest in something
_____ 6. sadness at not getting what you expect
_____ 7. non-professional
_____ 8. make late
_____ 9. give or throw to someone else
_____ 10. respect

a. match
b. amateur
c. enthusiasm
d. mad
e. delay
f. pass
g. champion
h. disappointment
i. admire
j. entire

E. Read the passage and answer the questions that follow.

This weekend there was a special television program on the 1986 European Championship Games. There was a variety of different sports, including running, jumping long distances, and jumping over a high bar with the help of a

5 pole. There were several different types of running contests:
(1) running long distances (2) running and jumping over a low
bar ("hurdles") and (3) running and passing a small bar to
other runners on the team ("relay races"). The best amateur
sportsmen in the world came to Stuttgart, Germany, to
10 compete. It rained the first day of the games, so
unfortunately the first matches were delayed. The audience
was, of course, disappointed, but not for very long. Daly
Thompson, the winner of several gold medals in the 1984
Olympics, competed in the ten-sport contest. The audience's
15 admiration for him was clear—the entire stadium yelled
enthusiastically every time he entered the field. Thompson
was never a very modest person, and his modesty did not
increase when he became the champion of the European
Championship Games!

1. Where were the European Championship Games held in 1986? _____

_____

2. What kinds of sports took place? _____

_____

3. Describe three kinds of running races. _____

_____

4. Were the games professional? _____

_____

5. Why was the audience disappointed? _____

_____

6. Who is Daly Thompson? _____

_____

7. How did the audience feel about Thompson? _____

_____

8. How did Thompson do at the games in Stuttgart? _____

_____

9. Did Thompson's modesty increase? _____

_____

Follow-up

F.   Dictation: Write the sentences that your teacher reads aloud.

1. _____

2. _____

3. _____

4. _____

5. _____

G.   Answer the following questions.

1. What government leader (or leaders) do you admire most? Why?
2. Name something about the United States that disappoints you.
3. Name something in your country that disappoints you.
4. What are the characteristics of a modest person?
5. What sports or games can you bet on?
6. Who are the champion sportsmen and women in your country?
7. What are some things that make you mad?
8. What are you most enthusiastic about in this school?
9. When do people need extra oxygen?
10. Name as many things as you can that you can catch.
11. What do you admire most about your parents?

Religion

Word Form Chart

NOUN	VERB	ADJECTIVE	ADVERB
			aloud
attendance	attend	attending	
belief	believe	believable	believably
believer		unbelievable	unbelievably
burial	bury	buried	
candle			
celebration	celebrate	celebrating	
faith		faithful	faithfully
		unfaithful	unfaithfully
festival		festival	
God			
god			
goddess			
grave			
heaven		heavenly	
heavens			
hell		hellish	
holiness		holy	
influence	influence	influential	influentially
		influenced	
		influencing	
miracle		miraculous	miraculously
Orient		Oriental	
prayer	pray	prayerful	
		praying	
religion		religious	religiously
sin	sin	sinful	sinfully
strictness		strict	strictly

Definitions and Examples

1. **believe** [to accept as true]

    Ancient man **believed** the earth was flat.
    Do you **believe** in ghosts?
    It is my **belief** that cats are unlucky.

2. **God** [the being that people believe is the maker and ruler of all things]

    Many people believe that **God** made the world.

    A: Do you believe in **God**?
    B: Yes. And I go to church every week.

3. **god** [a being considered superior to nature and humans; a being who some people think has special powers over the lives and activities of people]

    A goddess is a female **god**.
    When the **gods** were angry, the people were afraid.

4. **religion** [a system of belief in God or in a god; a system of values and practices]

    Some of the world's major religions are Buddhism, Christianity, Islam, Judaism, Hinduism, and Taoism.
    My family is not especially **religious**.

5. **pray** [to speak to God or to a god to give thanks or to ask for something]

    The people of the village **prayed** for an early end to the war.
    Unfortunately, their **prayers** were not answered.

6. **aloud** [using the voice]

    Please read your answer **aloud** so that the entire class can hear it.
    Some people say prayers silently; others say them **aloud**.

7. **attend** [to be at]

    Do you plan to **attend** his wedding?
    Attendance in history class is compulsory.

8. **bury** [to put a dead body or anything else in the ground and cover it]

    There is a special **burial** ground for military men.
    My grandfather is **buried** in the village where he was born.

9. **candle** [a thing that is burned to give light]

      Candles are useful if you have no electricity.
      Candles look nice on a formal dinner table.

10. **celebrate** [to honor a special day or event with ceremonies and other activities]

      The entire country **celebrated** the birth of the prince.
      The **celebration** included parties and a parade.

11. **faith** [a belief or trust; a religion]

      People of many different **faiths** live in this city.
      I have complete **faith** in this government.
      He served his captain **faithfully**.

12. **festival** [a celebration or holiday]

      Some religious **festivals** include family parties.
      Many countries have a **festival** to celebrate the beginning of a new
          year.

13. **holy** [related to God]

      A **holy** man serves God.
      You should be respectful when you visit a **holy** place.

14. **influence** [to cause a change in something or someone]

      A politician can **influence** many voters.
      Has religion been a big **influence** in your life?

15. **miracle** [something wonderful that cannot be explained by the laws of nature]

      The old woman said she had been cured by a **miracle**.
      The holy book contained many **miraculous** stories.

16. **Orient** [the countries of Asia or the East]

      China and Japan are **Oriental** countries.
      Did you enjoy your vacation in the **Orient**?

17. **grave** [a hole in the ground where a dead body is buried]

      Each year many people visit the **grave** of the president.
      We stood sadly at the side of the **grave**.

18. **heaven** [in some religions, the place where good people go when they die]

    Some people believe that gods and goddesses live in **heaven**.
    There is no sadness or pain in **heaven**.

19. **heavens** [the sky]

    The **heavens** contain the sun, the moon, and the stars.

20. **heavenly** [like heaven; happy, pleasant, and beautiful]

    This island is a **heavenly** place for a vacation.

21. **hell** [in some religions, the place where bad people go after they die]

    Hell is believed to be a very uncomfortable place.
    Famous artists have painted pictures of the fires of **hell**.

22. **sin** [to act in opposition to the wishes of God or the laws of a religion]

    Murder is a **sin** in many religions.
    The criminal said that he had **sinned** many times.

23. **strict** [following a rule or making others follow a rule in a careful way]

    Some religions are **stricter** than others.
    You should **strictly** follow your teacher's suggestions.

Introductory Exercises

A. Match each word with its definition.

_____ 1. a hole in the ground	**a.** aloud
_____ 2. a superior being	**b.** attend
_____ 3. using the voice	**c.** believe
_____ 4. something that gives light	**d.** bury
_____ 5. a system of belief	**e.** candle
_____ 6. to be at	**f.** grave
_____ 7. where God lives	**g.** god
_____ 8. to accept as true	**h.** heaven
_____ 9. related to God	**i.** holy
_____ 10. to speak to God	**j.** pray
	k. religion
	l. sin

B. Answer each question with a word from the word form chart in this unit.

1. What is a thing that cannot be explained by the laws of nature?
2. How do you honor a special day or event?
3. What do you do when you put a dead body in the ground?
4. What is an act in opposition to God?
5. Where do some people believe they go after they die? (two answers)
6. Where do some people believe God lives?
7. What is another word for religion?
8. What are the countries of Asia called?
9. What do you do when you talk to God?
10. What do you call a female god?

Study Exercises

C. Circle the word which is different in meaning.

1. festival   celebration   privacy
2. belief   faith   poison
3. beard   grave   hole
4. Oriental   hellish   eastern
5. acceptance   attendance   belief
6. prison   sky   heavens
7. strict   fancy   exact
8. occasionally   religiously   faithfully

D. Write **T** if the sentence is true and **F** if it is false.

_____ 1. Candles were used before the invention of electricity.
_____ 2. National celebrations often include military parades.
_____ 3. Parents often teach their children about religion.
_____ 4. Scientists have instruments for looking at the heavens.
_____ 5. Tourists often go to festivals.
_____ 6. Hell is believed to be very pleasant.
_____ 7. Miracles are so common that we see them every day.
_____ 8. Spain is an Oriental country.
_____ 9. Prayers are never said aloud.
_____ 10. Religion can influence how you think.

E.   In the blanks write the appropriate word from the word form chart in this unit.

1. Religion can _____ the history and politics of a country.
2. I follow the teachings of my religion very _____ .
3. The scientists discovered an ancient _____ ground.
4. In some religions, stealing is a(n) _____ .
5. We will _____ our fifth anniversary this year.
6. John _____-s church every week because he likes the music.
7. After a few years, grass and flowers grew on top of the soldier's _____ .
8. In some religions _____ is both powerful and loving.

F.   Read the following passage and answer the statements that follow.

There is no official religion in the United States. Instead, many religions are practiced by the different cultural groups that settled in the country. Some of these faiths are stricter than others, and some have more influence than others on
5   the daily lives of their members. Some religions have holy books that teach about sin and tell stories about miracles. Others have art and music as part of their long histories.

Most of the religions in the United States are based on a belief in God, but the festivals and celebrations are different
10   and interesting in each religion. For example, each religion has its own special ceremonies for important events such as births, marriages, deaths, and burials. Many religions require regular attendance at a church or other holy building, and the religious services sometimes include the lighting of candles
15   and the saying of prayers, either silently or aloud.

Write **T** if the sentence is true and **F** if it is false.

____ 1. The United States has one official religion.
____ 2. The religions in the United States are uniformly strict.
____ 3. Music and art have no place in these religions.
____ 4. A belief in God is common in the religions of the United States.
____ 5. All the religions have the same festivals and celebrations.
____ 6. Special ceremonies are different in each religion.
____ 7. Candles are used in some religious services.
____ 8. Prayers are read silently and never said aloud.

Follow-up

G. Dictation: Write the sentences that your teacher reads aloud.

    1. _____

    2. _____

    3. _____

    4. _____

    5. _____

H. Answer the following questions.

    1. What is the most common religion in your country?
    2. Do most of the people in your country attend regular religious services? When?
    3. Are most holidays religious holidays? Which ones?
    4. Are you from the Orient? If so, which country?
    5. Are there holy places in your city? Where? What do they look like?
    6. Does religion influence the politics of your country? How?
    7. Does the government have any influence on religion? How?
    8. Are most of the people in your country strict about their religion? What are some of the rules they follow?
    9. Do parents pray with their children in your country? When?
    10. Are there special burial places in your city? Where?

I. Describe a festival in your religion or in any religion in your country.

Education (B)

Word Form Chart

NOUN	VERB	ADJECTIVE	ADVERB	PREPOSITION
academic		academic	academically	
achievement	achieve			
athletics		athletic	athletically	
athlete				
			behind	behind
calculation	calculate	calculated		
calculator		calculating	calculatingly	
chance				
club				
community				
definition	define	defined		
		defining		
inside			inside	inside
kindness		kind	kindly	
		kindly		
laboratory				
line				
mind				
pupil				
scholarship				
scholar		scholarly		
		smart	smartly	
summary	summarize	summarized		
			then	
whisper	whisper	whispering		
		whispered		

Definitions and Examples

1. **laboratory** {informal: lab} [a room or building with special machines for doing scientific tests and research]

    We learned how to do experiments in the chemistry **laboratory**.
    Research scientists work in **labs**.

2. **academic** [relating to educational subjects, especially in higher education]

    Some students study subjects such as car repair or secretarial
        courses; other students study **academic** subjects such as physics
        or history because they want to go to college.
    John is doing well **academically** at the university, but he is still not
        used to living away from the family.

3. **athletic** [physically strong; of or for sports]

    John is very **athletic**. He can play almost any sport well.
    The **athletes** at our university, especially the football players,
        receive a lot of attention.
    The university built a new **athletic** building.
    They won many prizes in **athletic** competitions.

4. **behind** (a) [the place where someone has been]

    She left her shoes **behind**.
    When I got home I remembered that I had left my coat **behind**.

    (b) [in back of something]

    I was standing **behind** the door.

    A: Where is the chemistry building?
    B: It's **behind** the library.

5. **calculate** [to find out an answer using mathematics]

    They **calculated** that they needed four hours to drive from their
        home to the university.
    The students used a computer for their math **calculations**.

6. **calculator** [a machine used to make mathematical calculations]

    A: Are you permitted to use a **calculator** during your math tests?
    B: Yes. **Calculators** help us to solve the problems faster.

7. **chance** [something that happens unintentionally or without planning]

    I saw him by **chance** in the chemistry building.
    We had a **chance** meeting at the baseball game.

8. **inside** [the interior part; in the interior part]

   The **inside** of that school building is beautiful.
   The customers waited **inside** the store because of the bad weather.
   She stayed **inside** all day because she was sick.

9. **club** [a group of people who meet together regularly to do the same thing]

   The science **club** meets once a week to discuss new scientific discoveries.
   The members of the university Spanish **club** will travel to Spain next summer.

10. **community** [all the people who live in the same area]

    The people in our **community** attend all the athletic activities at the local high school.
    The academic **community** of a university consists of the professors and the students.

11. **whisper** [to speak very quietly]

    The children are not permitted to talk to each other in class, but sometimes they **whisper**.
    The teacher heard the pupils **whispering** during the exam.

12. **achieve** [to accomplish something]

    He **achieved** a high grade on his test.
    Mr. Jones is well-known for his many **achievements** in science.

13. **definition** [an explanation of the meaning of a word]

    You can find **definitions** of words in a dictionary.
    A: Can you **define** the word "zoology"?
    B: Yes. The **definition** of "zoology" is "the biological science of animals."

14. **kind** [helpful and pleasant]

    My uncle is very **kind**. He helped to pay for my tuition this year.
    The students liked their history professor because of his **kindness**.

15. **line** [a group of people or things standing one behind the other]

    The students must stand in **line** to get food in the cafeteria.
    There was a long **line** of students waiting to take the college entrance exam.

16. **scholar** [a person who studies seriously]

    That professor is a well-known **scholar** in biology.

17. **mind** (a) [the part of a human being that thinks, feels, learns, and remembers]

    Our teacher tells us to keep our **minds** on our work.
    Scientists do not completely understand how our **minds** work.

    (b) [an opinion]

    My sister always changes her **mind**.
    John and Mary both think Americans do not exercise enough; they are of the same **mind** on that subject.

18. **pupil** [a student]

    There are fifteen **pupils** in my English class.

    A: Mr. Smith, you have a telephone call.
    B: Who's calling?
    A: One of your **pupils**.

19. **scholarship** [the money won or given to a person to pay school or university costs]

    Ann won the **scholarship** because of her good grades.
    My **scholarship** will pay for tuition and dormitory costs for two years.

20. **smart** [intelligent]

    Joan is the **smartest** student in the physics class.

    A: My sister is really **smart**.
    B: Why do you say that?
    A: Because she passed a test and won a scholarship to study abroad.

21. **summary** [a short statement of the major ideas of a speech, article, or book]

    Our teacher asked us to write a **summary** of a chapter in our history book.
    Can you **summarize** the paragraph in a few words?

22. **then** (a) [at that time]

    I didn't know her **then**.

    A: Did you see Amy and Tom at 2:00?
    B: No. I didn't see them **then**.

    (b) [after that]

    We saw a movie, and **then** we went to the dormitory.
    First I studied chemistry, and **then** I studied engineering.

Introductory Exercises

A. Match the word with its definition.

_____ **1.** all the people who live in the same area

_____ **2.** helpful

_____ **3.** a room/building with special machines for tests and research

_____ **4.** to accomplish

_____ **5.** the part of the body that thinks, learns, etc.

_____ **6.** an explanation of the meaning of a word

_____ **7.** money won or given to pay for school costs

_____ **8.** to find out an answer using math

_____ **9.** intelligent

_____ **10.** a student

_____ **11.** to speak quietly

_____ **12.** the happening of something that is not planned

_____ **13.** at that time

_____ **14.** a row of people or things

_____ **15.** a group of people who meet together to do the same thing

a. achieve
b. behind
c. calculate
d. chance
e. club
f. community
g. definition
h. inside
i. kind
j. laboratory
k. line
l. mind
m. pupil
n. scholarship
o. smart
p. then
q. whisper

B. Substitute a word from the word form chart for the underlined word(s) in each sentence.

1. There were only a few <u>students</u> who knew the answer to the question.
2. John waited for three hours; <u>after that</u> he went home.
3. Joan is very <u>intelligent</u>. She received the highest grade in biology class.
4. If students want to talk in the library, they should <u>speak softly</u>.
5. Can you <u>tell me the meaning of</u> that word?
6. Her father's company gave her the <u>money to pay for university costs</u>.
7. My new roommate is very <u>helpful and pleasant</u>.

8. Our homework was to write a <u>short statement of the major ideas</u> of the story in French.
9. My brother is <u>physically strong</u>. He plays basketball and football and runs every day.

Study Exercises

C. Match the words that have similar meanings.

___ 1. achieve   **a.** group
___ 2. behind   **b.** brain
___ 3. club   **c.** back of
___ 4. definition   **d.** intelligent
___ 5. kind   **e.** nice
___ 6. mind   **f.** student
___ 7. pupil   **g.** succeed
___ 8. smart   **h.** explanation

D. Match the words that have opposite meanings.

___ 1. achieve   **a.** teacher
___ 2. behind   **b.** now
___ 3. pupil   **c.** stupid
___ 4. smart   **d.** scream
___ 5. then   **e.** fail
___ 6. whisper   **f.** unpleasant
___ 7. kind   **g.** in front

E. Write **T** if the answer is true and **F** if it is false.

___ 1. A pupil teaches in a university.
___ 2. Scientists often work in laboratories.
___ 3. A scholar is usually smart.
___ 4. Most people like to stand in line.
___ 5. Sports are academic activities.
___ 6. Students should whisper if they must talk in the library.

_____ 7. Graduating from college is an achievement.

_____ 8. Calculators help students to solve math problems.

_____ 9. Summaries are calculations.

_____ 10. Rich students need scholarships.

F. In the blanks, write the appropriate word(s) from the word form chart in this unit.

1. I met Professor Jones by _____ when I was downtown.

2. Several _____-s were absent on the day of the test.

3. Sometimes it is difficult to find the correct _____ of a word.

4. That university is famous for its _____ excellence in computer science.

5. I found my pencil _____ my book.

6. Students stand in _____ every semester to buy their books.

7. We waited for our friends _____ the campus book store.

8. Many young women and men win _____ scholarships because of their ability to compete in sports.

9. First, we attended the physics lecture; _____ we went to lunch.

10. Bill is the _____-est student in our math class. He always gets "A's" on his tests.

11. The German _____ will meet on Friday to plan a party for new members.

12. Professor Black is a(n) _____ who is famous for his achievements in medicine.

13. Sometimes it is difficult to keep your _____ on your studies.

14. My professor is very _____ . She told us about many books we could read for our test, and she also gave us extra help in studying for it.

G. Read the passage and answer the questions that follow.

There are many different kinds of scholarships available in the United States to help students pay tuition, dormitory, and other costs at the university level. Students who need help paying for these costs must first apply for a scholarship.
5 Usually a student must complete an application, take an

examination, and/or write an essay. Applicants are also asked to state their community activities, interests, club memberships, and other academic or non-academic achievements.

10 Government and community groups offer academic scholarships only to those students who have good grades and meet various other requirements. Universities offer both academic and athletic scholarships to those students with athletic abilities. These students then play on various university athletic teams: football, basketball, volleyball,

15 soccer, swimming, etc.

Since college expenses are so high, many students might not have the chance to study. Scholarships provide this chance to students who are unable to pay the cost of a good university education.

Write **T** if the sentence is true and **F** if it is false.

_____ **1.** Anyone can get an academic scholarship.

_____ **2.** A student must apply for a scholarship.

_____ **3.** Universities offer only athletic scholarships.

_____ **4.** Only students with good grades can get academic scholarships.

_____ **5.** Students who win academic scholarships always play on university athletic teams.

Answer the questions.

6. What kinds of costs do scholarships pay for? _____

_____

7. Which groups offer scholarships? _____

_____

8. How does a student apply for a scholarship? _____

_____

9. What kinds of students apply for scholarships? _____

_____

10. Why are scholarships advantageous? _____

_____

Follow-up

H. Dictation: Write the sentences that your teacher reads aloud.

1. _____

2. _____

3. _____

4. _____

5. _____

I. Answer the following questions.

  1. When do people usually whisper?
  2. Name some academic subjects that students study in high school.
  3. Have you had a chance to travel to many foreign countries?
  4. What types of scholarships are available at your school?
  5. When do you have difficulty keeping your mind on your studies?
  6. Are athletics very important in your school? In your community?
  7. What is your highest achievement in school? In life?
  8. Do you use calculators in math or other classes?
  9. Are you a member of any academic clubs? Which ones?
10. Do you have to stand in line in your school? When?

J. Talk about one of the following subjects:

1. Describe the community in which you live.
2. Describe how a student can get a scholarship in your country.

Work (B)

Word Form Chart

NOUN	VERB	ADJECTIVE	ADVERB
announcement	announce	announced	
announcer			
career			
corporation	incorporate	corporate	
dependence	depend	dependent	dependently
independence		independent	independently
dismissal	dismiss	dismissed	
eagerness		eager	eagerly
	fix	fixed	
initiation	initiate	initial	initially
luck		lucky	luckily
		unlucky	unluckily
resignation	resign	resigning	
strike	strike (struck, struck)	striking	
suddenness		sudden	suddenly
support	support	supporting	
		supported	
		supportive	supportively
technique		technical	technically
warning	warn	warning	

Definitions and Examples

1. **fix** [to repair]

   > He needs tools to **fix** the car that does not start.
   > The store offered to **fix** my broken watch.
   > It works well now that it has been **fixed**.

2. **announce** [to tell to people]

   > The boss **announced** an increase in wages.
   > The government **announced** that unemployment had increased.
   > We were surprised by his **announcement** that he was quitting.

3. **initially** [at first]

   > **Initially** she liked her new job, but after a few months, she began to hate it.
   > His **initial** eagerness to work changed quickly to boredom with the job.

4. **dismiss** [to take a job away from a person]

   > The boss **dismissed** him because he did not do his job well.
   > She argued with her employer about her **dismissal**.

5. **resign** [to quit a job]

   > He **resigned** because he did not like his job.
   > She **resigned** from her old job so that she could take a better one that had been offered to her.
   > She gave the boss her **resignation** letter.

6. **strike** [a situation in which workers as a group refuse to work, usually to get higher wages or better working conditions]

   > When the company did not increase their wages, the workers went on **strike**.
   > The **strike** lasted for two weeks before the workers returned to work.

7. **support** [to help someone to exist or to do something, often with money]

   > That man is **supporting** a wife and three children.
   > All of the workers are **supporting** the strike; none of them went to work today.
   > My parents **supported** me while I was in college.
   > The legs of a table **support** it.

8. **career** [a job, requiring training, that a person holds for a long time]

   His **career** as a lawyer earned him a lot of money.
   She had a twenty-year **career** as a teacher.

9. **eager** [wanting to do something very much]

   Workers are always **eager** for pay day.
   She **eagerly** waited for 5:00, when she could go home.

10. **corporation** [a company owned by a group of people]

   Many large **corporations** have offices in major cities around the
     world.
   She is a lawyer for a **corporation** based in New York.

11. **dependent** [needing support from someone else or something else]

   That new man is very **dependent**; he always asks for help
     with each job.
   The success of the factory **depends** on the workers.
   The salesmen for this company have to be **independent** and find
     new people to sell to.
   Depending on how much he sells, his earnings will increase.

12. **luck** [the power which some people believe brings good or bad fortune]

   With **luck**, that company will succeed.
   Some people think that black cats are not **lucky**.

   A: Do you believe in **luck**?
   B: No. I believe in hard work.

13. **technical** [requiring specialized information, especially scientific
    information]

   That job required **technical** training.
   This book describes many difficult **techniques** that I cannot
     understand.

14. **warn** [to tell someone that something bad may happen]

   The boss **warned** him that he would be dismissed if he were late
     again.
   The **warning** scared him, and he began to arrive on time.

15. **sudden** [surprising; without advance warning; abrupt]

   His **sudden** resignation surprised everyone.
   Her **sudden** unemployment was very stressful; she had had no time
     to prepare for it.
   I jumped when a bell rang **suddenly** in the silence.

Introductory Exercises

A. Match each word with its definition.

_____ **1.** a company owned by a group of people	**a.** announce
_____ **2.** to repair	**b.** career
_____ **3.** at first	**c.** corporation
_____ **4.** requiring specialized information	**d.** dependent
_____ **5.** needing support from someone or something	**e.** dismiss
	f. eager
_____ **6.** to help someone to exist or to do something	**g.** fix
	h. initially
_____ **7.** wanting very much to do something	**i.** luck
	j. resign
_____ **8.** to take a job away from a person	**k.** strike
	l. sudden
_____ **9.** without advance warning	**m.** support
_____ **10.** to tell the public	**n.** technical
_____ **11.** to quit a job	**o.** warn

B. Answer each question with a word from the word form chart in this unit.

   1. What are many large companies?
   2. What does an employer do to a bad employee?
   3. What might workers do when their pay is too low?
   4. What can an employee do if he hates his job?
   5. What does the government do with important news?
   6. What should you do with something which is broken?
   7. What should you do when you see people in danger?
   8. What do most students in universities prepare for?
   9. What do parents do for their children?
  10. What can you call something which surprises you?
  11. What is a way of doing something using special knowledge?

Study Exercises

C. Write **T** if the sentence is true and **F** if it is false.

_____ 1. Secret things are announced.

_____ 2. We fix things which are broken.

_____ 3. People depend on their jobs for support.

_____ 4. The owners of companies enjoy strikes.

_____ 5. Bosses dismiss good workers.

_____ 6. People who do not like their jobs may resign.

_____ 7. An initial problem happens at the beginning.

_____ 8. People are eager for things that they do not like.

_____ 9. If something happens suddenly, it may surprise people.

_____ 10. People want lucky things.

D. In the blanks, write the appropriate word(s) from the word form chart in this unit.

1. The workers _____ -ed to the owner that they would go

   on _____ unless they got higher wages.

2. He resigned after a twenty-year _____ with that company.

3. I did not like my job _____ , but now I love it.

4. For some people, black cats and the number thirteen mean bad

   _____ .

5. Those two companies are _____ of each other; they are not related.

6. That corporation _____ -s many people, if you count the workers and their families.

7. The company _____ -ed him because he made too many mistakes in his work.

8. She was _____ to begin her new job; she wanted to start as soon as possible.

9. His dismissal from the company _____ ; he had no warning.

E. Read the passage and answer the questions that follow.

The end of a three-month old strike against the Green Corporation was announced yesterday. The strike had begun after the sudden dismissal of a group of workers. The rest of the workers immediately went on strike in support of their
5 jobless co-workers. The major complaint of the striking workers was that no warning was given to their friends who had been dismissed.

The attitude of the corporation was that, with the current business problems, it was necessary to dismiss some
10 of the workers, and that those who were dismissed were simply unlucky. Initially, the company warned the strikers that they were only hurting their careers with their actions. However, as the corporation saw how the strike was hurting their business, they became more eager to negotiate with the
15 striking workers and come to a solution. Both sides announced their approval of the results of the negotiations, and said that the factory would be in full operation by this afternoon.

1. What caused the strike? _____

_____

2. What were the dismissed workers not given? _____

_____

3. How did the corporation describe the dismissed workers? _____

_____

4. What made the corporation eager to talk to the strikers? _____

_____

5. How did the strikers feel about the negotiated solution? _____

_____

Follow-up

F. Dictation: Write the sentences that your teacher reads aloud.

1. _____

2. _____

3. _____

4. _____

5. _____

G. Answer the following questions.

1. What type of career are you planning?
2. How does the government of your country make major announcements?
3. Do parents in your country want their children to be dependent or independent? Why?
4. What things are workers usually eager for?
5. What jobs require technical training? Do those jobs pay well in your country?
6. What kinds of workers often go on strike in your country? Why? Are all workers permitted to strike?
7. Have you ever resigned from a job? Why? Do people in your country often resign from jobs?
8. Are you supporting yourself now? Are you supporting anyone else? Who?
9. Do you believe in luck? What things do you think are lucky for you?

H. Give some reasons why . . .

1. a person might resign from a job.
2. a person might be dismissed from a job.
3. workers might go on strike.

Business

Word Form Chart

NOUN	VERB	ADJECTIVE	ADVERB	CONJUNCTION
customer				
defect		defective		
factor				
goods				
			hardly	
inflation	inflate	inflated		
		inflationary		
occasion		occasional	occasionally	
		ordinary	ordinarily	
		extraordinary	extraordinarily	
				otherwise
period		periodic	periodically	
periodical				
profit	profit	profitable	profitably	
			quite	
request	request	requested		
		slight	slightly	
				unless
wisdom		wise	wisely	

Definitions and Examples

1. **customer** [a person who buys something]

    The **customers** in the computer store were looking for quality and low price.
    Some **customers** are never satisfied with their purchases.

2. **defect** [a weakness]

    There is a **defect** in this sweater; one arm is longer than the other.
    A clock with a twisted hand is **defective**.

3. **factor** [a condition or quality that causes something to happen]

    Hard work is an important **factor** in success.
    What **factors** are responsible for an increased divorce rate?

4. **goods** [the things that are sold; the things that belong to someone]

    That store sells high quality **goods**.
    All of our household **goods** were damaged in the flood.

5. **hardly** [only just; almost not]

    I can **hardly** see the trees through the fog.
    We **hardly** started our picnic when it started to rain.
    I got up so late that I **hardly** had time for breakfast.

6. **inflate** (a) [to cause to get bigger]

    Can you help me **inflate** these balloons?

    (b) [increasing prices]

    High **inflation** is not good for business.

7. **occasion** [a time when something happens; an important or special happening]

    I know I have heard this music before, but I cannot remember the **occasion**.
    Their anniversary party was a happy **occasion**.

8. **occasional** [happening infrequently]

    We expect **occasional** rain today.
    I attend concerts only **occasionally**.

9. **ordinary** [common; regular; usual; not different from the others]

    I thought her dress was very **ordinary**.
    We **ordinarily** eat lunch in the cafeteria.

10. **extraordinary** [very unusual]

   A trip around the world is an **extraordinary** journey.
   My family is **extraordinary**; I have twelve sisters.

11. **otherwise** [in other ways; or else; if not]

   He got sick on the airplane; **otherwise**, his vacation was fun.
   Please be quiet; **otherwise**, I will have to ask you to leave.

12. **period** [a length of time]

   An hour is a **period** of sixty minutes.
   He visited us for only a short **period**.
   My mother calls me **periodically**—usually on the weekend.

13. **periodical** [a magazine that is printed at regular times]

   The **periodicals** are kept in a special room in the library.
   I used both books and **periodicals** to write this research paper.

14. **profit** [the earnings of a business after the expenses have been paid]

   It's a small store, but it makes a good **profit**.
   You cannot **profit** from foolish business practices.

15. **quite** [very completely; really]

   The wind is **quite** strong today.
   His grades were not **quite** good enough.
   We had **quite** a party for my birthday.

16. **request** [to ask or ask for]

   His landlady **requested** that he pay the rent on time.
   My employer did not like my **request** for higher pay.

17. **slight** [small; not much; not important]

   She was a very **slight** child, not at all like her heavy brother.
   There has been only a **slight** improvement in the weather this
     week.
   The population has increased **slightly** since last year.

18. **unless** [if not]

   We will have a majority **unless** you change your vote.
   Unless I pass this test, I will fail the course.

19. **wisdom** [good judgement based on experience]

   Our captain showed both **wisdom** and bravery.
   The **wise** old woman gave us good advice.

Introductory Exercises

A. Match each word with its definition.

_____	**1.** a length of time	**a.** customer
_____	**2.** only just	**b.** defect
_____	**3.** happening infrequently	**c.** factor
_____	**4.** small	**d.** hardly
_____	**5.** a weakness	**e.** inflate
_____	**6.** to increase in size or amount	**f.** occasional
_____	**7.** common	**g.** ordinary
_____	**8.** to ask	**h.** period
_____	**9.** good judgement	**i.** profit
_____	**10.** a person who buys	**j.** request
		k. slight
		l. wisdom

B. Answer each question with a word from the word form chart in this unit.

1. What do we call things that are sold?
2. What are a minute, a day, and a year examples of?
3. What does a business owner hope to have after the expenses have been paid?
4. What is another word for "ask"?
5. How might you describe a small woman?
6. What do you have if you can make good decisions about right and wrong?
7. What do we call a thing that is common?
8. What do we do to a soccer ball that needs air?
9. What does a book with missing pages have?
10. Who are the people who buy things?

Study Exercises

C. Write **T** if the sentence is true and **F** if it is false.

_____ **1.** A century is a short period of time.

_____ **2.** A farmer should use safe tools; otherwise, he could be injured.

_____ **3.** A dozen is not quite twelve.

_____ 4. Unless animals have air, they cannot live.

_____ 5. Strength is an important factor in athletic success.

_____ 6. The goods in a store are not for sale.

_____ 7. A graduation is a happy occasion.

_____ 8. Very high inflation is good for business.

_____ 9. A kilometer is slightly longer than an inch.

_____ 10. A wise man makes good use of his intelligence.

D. In the blanks, write the appropriate word(s) from the word form chart in this unit.

1. Regular cleaning is an important _____ in dental health.

2. A basketball game has four _____ -s .

3. Buy your tickets early; _____ , they may not be available.

4. A nightmare is not a(n) _____ dream. Most people only have nightmares occasionally.

5. You should _____ an application if you want them to send one to you.

6. In many places you cannot buy beer _____ you are 21 years old.

7. Does your company sell _____ or services?

8. The forecast is for similar weather tomorrow; it will be _____ warmer.

9. I returned the fan to the store because it was _____ .

10. Because older people have more experience, they are generally _____ -er than younger people.

E. Circle the word which is different.

1. profit   earnings   suicide

2. little   quite   completely

3. slight   sequence   small

4. common   ordinary   unusual

5. marine   inflate   increase

6. request   ask   casual

7. magazine   emphasis   periodical

8. buyer   customer   attempt

F.   Read the passage and answer the questions that follow.

> Three years ago, Andy graduated from college with a
> degree in business and a specialty in international banking.
> Andy wanted to start his own import company. He liked the
> idea of making periodic trips to foreign countries to buy
> 5 extraordinary objects and of selling them at home for a profit.
> Andy's father was quite worried about him, though,
> because he had hardly any practical experience. Andy knew
> about the factors that cause inflation, for example, but he
> probably did not know how to deal with defective goods and
> 10 occasional angry customers who requested their money back.
> His father said that Andy had knowledge but not wisdom.
> But that was three years ago. Today Andy's company is
> very successful. He actually made $135,000 in profit, and
> unless inflation continues to rise, he may even decide to
> 15 expand the business.

1. When did Andy graduate from college? _____

_____

2. What did Andy study in university? _____

_____

3. What kind of business does Andy have? _____

_____

4. Why did he decide on this type of business? _____

_____

5. Why was Andy's father worried about him? _____

_____

6. What is an example of what Andy knew about? _____

_____

7. What are two examples of what Andy did not know about? _____

_____

8. Is Andy's company profitable now? How much profit did he make?

_____

9. What might Andy do with his business? _____

_____

10. What might make him decide not to expand his business? _____

_____

Follow-up

G. Dictation: Write the sentences that your teacher reads aloud.

1. _____

2. _____

3. _____

4. _____

5. _____

H. Answer the following questions.

1. What period of history do you think is the most interesting? Why?
2. What kind of transportation is ordinary in your country?
3. What goods are difficult to find in your country?
4. What are the important factors in a happy marriage?
5. What kind of business makes the largest profits in your country?
6. What periodicals do you read regularly?
7. Is the rate of inflation high now?
8. What factors influence inflation?
9. What special occasions do you celebrate in your country?
10. What can you do if you buy a defective tool?

I. Explain . . .

1. the factors that a customer thinks about before he buys something.
2. the factors that a seller thinks about before he puts a price on something he wants to sell.

Answer Key

Unit 1

C. 1. F 2. T 3. T 4. F 5. T 6. F 7. F 8. T 9. T

D. 1. however 2. attention 3. novels 4. praises 5. almost 6. lecture
7. rules 8. review

E. 1. A good student receives praise. 2. Please review the grammar rules.
3. The seminar meets at 9:00. 4. Exercise is necessary for good health.
5. Pay attention to the teacher.

F. 1. T 2. T 3. T 4. F 5. F 6. F 7. F

Unit 2

C. 1. j 2. i 3. h 4. g 5. b 6. a 7. c 8. e 9. d 10. f

D. 1. occupation 2. stress 3. accomplishment 4. negotiations
5. manufactured 6. at once 7. offered 8. executives 9. complicated
10. increase

E. 1. tired of his occupation 2. how complicated everything was 3. negotiate
with banks to get a loan 4. the bank executive at National Bank 5. find a
small building to buy or rent 6. The author and his friend described how they
wanted it to look. 7. They wanted to increase the cost. 8. They had already
negotiated a contract. 9. bought tables and chairs from a manufacturer
10. They offered good salaries. 11. John would be the executive responsible
for business. His friend would manage the preparation of food and the staff.
12. stressed; Business was slow and they lacked money. 13. helped to
increase business 14. It is their biggest accomplishment.

Unit 3

C. 1. to arrive 2. vehicle 3. exit 4. load 5. motor

D. 1. size 2. signals 3. loads 4. directions 5. vehicles 6. speeds

E. **1.** Highways with a number ending in 0, 2, 4, 6, or 8 go in an east–west direction. Highways numbered with 1, 3, 5, 7, 9 go north and south. **2.** to show that the highway circles a city **3.** The exit name and number is on a sign above the road. **4.** The exit lane is also the entrance lane. **5.** use turn signals **6.** 65 miles/hr. It is different on exits and entrances and in heavily populated areas. **7.** Motorists should wear safety belts, never throw anything out the car windows, drive within the speed limit, and pay attention to traffic signals.

F. ACROSS: **4.** via **5.** inspection **7.** truck **10.** transportation **11.** speed **12.** reason **13.** vehicle **16.** passengers
DOWN: **1.** backward **2.** continue **3.** motorist **6.** exit **8.** journey **9.** signal **14.** hole **15.** load

Unit 4

C. **1.** unfashionable **2.** impractical **3.** unpopular **4.** unsuitable **5.** unaltered
1. d **2.** b **3.** e **4.** c **5.** a

D. **1.** F **2.** T **3.** T **4.** T **5.** F **6.** T **7.** T **8.** T **9.** F **10.** T

E. **1.** loose **2.** appearance **3.** genuine **4.** fit **5.** fancy/fashionable/popular **6.** fashion **7.** popular **8.** spots **9.** remove **10.** altered **11.** practical

F. **1.** fancy **2.** bargain **3.** genuine **4.** practical **5.** spot **6.** customary

G. **1.** a fancy party **2.** It was the only suitable dress she had. **3.** perfectly **4.** no **5.** at a fashionable restaurant **6.** young popular singers **7.** the latest fashions, a beautiful long fur coat, a dress of genuine leather **8.** A piece of cake fell on her dress and made a big spot. **9.** removed it with soap and water

Unit 5

C. **1.** die **2.** coast **3.** gloves **4.** army **5.** enough **6.** supply **7.** damage

D. **1.** contact **2.** route **3.** abruptly **4.** seconds **5.** miles **6.** copy **7.** stick

E. **1.** F **2.** T **3.** T **4.** T **5.** F **6.** T **7.** F **8.** T

F. **1.** F **2.** T **3.** T **4.** T **5.** F **6.** T **7.** T

Unit 6

D. **1.** F **2.** T **3.** T **4.** F **5.** T **6.** F **7.** F **8.** F

E. **1.** expand **2.** forever **3.** devise, drill **4.** real, permanently **5.** bottom **6.** below, surface **7.** volume **8.** estimate **9.** separate, layers **10.** substance

F. **1.** problem **2.** drill **3.** change **4.** expand **5.** layer **6.** problem **7.** substance

G. **1.** F **2.** T **3.** F **4.** T **5.** F **6.** F

Unit 7

C. **1.** T **2.** F **3.** F **4.** T **5.** F **6.** F **7.** T **8.** F **9.** F

D. **1.** g **2.** d **3.** i **4.** a **5.** e **6.** j **7.** f **8.** c

E.   **1.** writes book reviews for the town newspaper   **2.** The conclusions are revealed too early.   **3.** non-fiction books in which the author's attitude is strongly negative or positive; He feels a book is not convincing if only one side of the story is given.   **4.** biographies and historical fiction; learns many things through reading them.

Unit 8

D.   **1.** F   **2.** T   **3.** T   **4.** F   **5.** F   **6.** F   **7.** F   **8.** T   **9.** T   **10.** T   **11.** T

E.   **1.** intend   **2.** toward   **3.** envious   **4.** accustomed to   **5.** casual   **6.** afford   **7.** rises   **8.** rush   **9.** sights (views)   **10.** deserves   **11.** view   **12.** equal   **13.** altitudes   **14.** expedition

F.   **1.** rise   **2.** envy   **3.** equal   **4.** view   **5.** rush   **6.** last   **7.** sight

G.   **1.** F   **2.** T   **3.** T   **4.** F   **5.** F   **6.** T   **7.** T   **8.** F   **9.** T   **10.** F   **11.** F   **12.** The weather at high altitudes is cold.   **13.** the sunset, fields, trees, hills, valleys   **14.** He had to work.

Unit 9

C.   **1.** F   **2.** F   **3.** T   **4.** F   **5.** T   **6.** F   **7.** T   **8.** F   **9.** T   **10.** T   **11.** F

D.   **1.** d   **2.** i   **3.** e   **4.** a   **5.** g   **6.** h   **7.** f   **8.** c

E.   **1.** by suicide   **2.** the main safe   **3.** He had not locked the safe.   **4.** with poison   **5.** He could not live with the embarrassment.   **6.** forgiveness from the people whose money had been stolen

Unit 10

C.   **1.** F   **2.** T   **3.** T   **4.** T   **5.** F   **6.** T   **7.** F   **8.** F   **9.** T   **10.** F   **11.** F   **12.** F   **13.** T

D.   **1.** mass   **2.** telescope   **3.** research   **4.** metric   **5.** acid   **6.** geology   **7.** telescope   **8.** fill

E.   **1.** acid   **2.** research   **3.** massive   **4.** marine   **5.** questionnaire   **6.** zero   **7.** rockets   **8.** crushed   **9.** powder   **10.** metric   **11.** incredible

Unit 11

C.   **1.** F   **2.** T   **3.** F   **4.** T   **5.** T   **6.** T   **7.** T   **8.** F   **9.** F   **10.** F   **11.** F   **12.** F   **13.** T

D.   **1.** b   **2.** g   **3.** e   **4.** f   **5.** h   **6.** a   **7.** i

E.   **1.** reluctant   **2.** harsh/severe   **3.** severely   **4.** mind   **5.** thunder/lightning   **6.** lightning/thunder   **7.** wet   **8.** humid   **9.** oranges   **10.** continent

F.   **1.** in the Middle East   **2.** arid   **3.** near oases (water holes)   **4.** sand and rock hills   **5.** no   **6.** in the interior of South America   **7.** tropical   **8.** because of heavy rains, many floods, and very humid air   **9.** 40–60 inches a year   **10.** plants that are not usable

Unit 12

C.   **1.** activity   **2.** nightmare   **3.** smoothly   **4.** mental, physical   **5.** shallow   **6.** numerous   **7.** burst   **8.** fantasy   **9.** ghost (nightmarish)   **10.** slid

D. **1.** She/he was holding a big round ballon. Suddenly it burst. **2.** The two people (friends, a boy and a girl) are sitting on the edge (side) of the fountain. The water is shooting high into the air. A small bird is standing on the edge of the fountain. It is probably going to get a drink of water. **3.** The man is having a nightmare. He is dreaming that two frightening ghosts are running after him trying to get him. He can't wait to wake up. **4.** The broken bowl needs to be glued back together. I'll put glue on both of the broken edges and hold the piece smoothly in place until the glue dries.

E. **1.** T **2.** F **3.** T **4.** T **5.** T **6.** T **7.** F **8.** F **9.** T **10.** F

F. **1.** It offers numerous outdoor activities and ceremonies. **2.** There are movies, music, theater and magic, for example. **3.** Children can take part in creative activities. **4.** They can go to different locations to paint, make models, and sing. **5.** Physical exercise includes ballet, tennis, and other sports. **6.** Academic classes give them science, writing, reading, or math. **7.** The city got a new fountain for its 200th anniversary. **8.** The fountain shows the city's accomplishments. The water shoots high from the center. There are lights in a shallow area filled with water. **9.** The mayor presented the fountain during an official evening ceremony. **10.** The ceremony consisted of speeches, music, and other entertainment. **11.** A band played loudly, and balloons rose into the air when the mayor turned the water on. **12.** They stayed there to enjoy the fountain, to listen to music, and to watch other anniversary activities.

Unit 13

C. **1.** F **2.** T **3.** F **4.** F **5.** T **6.** T **7.** F **8.** F **9.** T **10.** T **11.** T

D. **1.** g **2.** e **3.** d **4.** a **5.** b **6.** i **7.** f

E. **1.** (a) a decrease in robberies (b) do not need to make as many withdrawals (c) can place orders by phone **2.** so he does not have to pay interest **3.** The bill does not arrive until the end of the month.

Unit 14

C. **1.** approve **2.** emotions **3.** kiss **4.** blond **5.** rely **6.** infant **7.** beard **8.** misbehave **9.** discussion **10.** belong **11.** angry

D. **1.** T **2.** F **3.** T **4.** F **5.** T **6.** T **7.** F **8.** F **9.** T **10.** T

E. **1.** an adult **2.** no **3.** so that he did not have to rely on anyone **4.** (a) so that his parents could not disapprove of his actions (b) so that his parents could not get angry with him (c) so that his parents could not ask him questions (d) so that everything in the apartment would belong to him **5.** He sees that his thoughts were infantile. **6.** Independence is difficult. **7.** a dependent child

F. **1.** They were active and not always well-behaving. **2.** She disapproved. **3.** arguments **4.** put dirty water on a neighbor's blond hair **5.** tried to discuss the situation first **6.** his "beard" **7.** looked at them disapprovingly **8.** She borrowed her sister's dress without permission and got juice on it. **9.** She screamed angrily, saying the author was unreliable and infantile. **10.** very emotional **11.** She kissed her.

Unit 15

C. 1. burn 2. beef 3. talk 4. knife

D. 1. sharp 2. tasted 3. bottle 4. ham 5. butter 6. containers 7. touch
8. dozen 9. smelled

E. 1. so that it stays fresh and does not make people ill 2. so that no dust, dirt,
or dirty water comes into contact with the food 3. in closed containers in the
refrigerator 4. if it looks or smells bad 5. It will not keep the food cool.

F. 1. Keep them clean and in good working condition. Keep the inside of the
refrigerator free from ice. 2. Keep knives in a knife holder. Wash knives
separately. Store dishes and glass containers carefully so that none break.
3. Keep pot handles away from the edge of the stove when cooking. 4. Be
prepared for accidents. Keep a bag of flour near the stove. Run cool water over
burns. Keep telephone numbers nearby.

Unit 16

C. 1. f 2. h 3. i 4. j 5. g 6. a 7. b 8. c 9. e 10. d

D. 1. elevator 2. knock 3. damp 4. due 5. dust 6. carpets (carpeting)
7. per 8. welcome

E. ACROSS: 1. vacant 3. due 5. elevator 6. step 8. carpet 11. housing
12. gate 15. interior 16. knock
DOWN: 2. attached 3. dusty 4. deposit 7. per 8. ceiling 9. ruin
10. dampness 13. rear 14. porch

F. 1. knock at the door 2. to the rear of the house 3. a small yard surrounded
by a fence with an old metal gate 4. It was vacant. 5. It had water
damage. 6. in good condition but dusty 7. to see who they were; The house
belonged to him. 8. $350 per month, due on the fifth day of each month
9. If they repaired the ceiling, he would not charge them a deposit.

Unit 17

C. 1. F 2. F 3. T 4. T 5. T 6. T 7. F 8. F 9. T 10. T 11. T 12. T

D. 1. double 2. provision 3. source 4. dig 5. dam 6. cage 7. irrigate

E. 1. a farming village 2. provides the water for irrigation 3. over forty years
ago 4. does not hold enough water 5. more than double the water they have
now 6. a new dam, immediately 7. They promised to build the new dam
before the next planting season.

Unit 18

C. 1. F 2. T 3. T 4. T 5. F 6. F 7. T 8. F 9. F 10. T

D. 1. d 2. a 3. g 4. l 5. j 6. b 7. h 8. f

E. 1. a majority 2. an informal agreement 3. several weeks 4. oppose it 5. It
will fail because it will not produce more jobs in the country. 6. by political
games

Unit 19

C. **1.** birth **2.** brain **3.** twisted **4.** chest **5.** normal (abnormal) **6.** seems **7.** thermometer

D. **1.** T **2.** T **3.** F **4.** T **5.** F **6.** T **7.** F **8.** T **9.** F

E. ACROSS: **1.** chest **4.** birth **6.** brain **8.** recent **9.** seem **10.** glasses **12.** alive **13.** knee **14.** normal
DOWN: **2.** heart **3.** thermometer **5.** twist **7.** neck **11.** skin **12.** ankle

F. **1.** in the emergency room of a big city hospital **2.** in a taxi **3.** a serious heart abnormality **4.** a broken knee, a neck injury **5.** a baseball player **6.** pains in her chest **7.** Yes. He seems happy.

Unit 20

C. **1.** F **2.** F **3.** F **4.** F **5.** T **6.** T **7.** F **8.** T **9.** T **10.** T

D. **1.** invade **2.** village **3.** offer **4.** opposite **5.** level **6.** obvious **7.** sand **8.** proceed

E. **1.** brave **2.** invade **3.** scarce **4.** crew **5.** captain **6.** selection **7.** citizens **8.** duty

F. **1.** an army captain in World War II **2.** France **3.** in an explosion **4.** She fell asleep. **5.** She describes the battles and capture of the capital. **6.** joins the citizens for a parade and party **7.** his army uniform

Unit 21

C. **1.** F **2.** F **3.** T **4.** F **5.** T **6.** T **7.** F **8.** T **9.** F **10.** F **11.** F **12.** F

D. **1.** g **2.** d **3.** j **4.** a **5.** c **6.** h **7.** b **8.** e **9.** f **10.** i

E. **1.** Stuttgart, Germany **2.** a variety including running and jumping **3.** long distance; running and passing a small bar to another person; running and jumping over a low bar **4.** no **5.** It rained, and the first matches were delayed. **6.** the winner of several gold medals in the 1984 Olympics **7.** admiring and enthusiastic **8.** He was the champion. **9.** no

Unit 22

C. **1.** privately **2.** poison **3.** beard **4.** hellish **5.** attendance **6.** prison **7.** fancy **8.** occasionally

D. **1.** T **2.** T **3.** T **4.** T **5.** T **6.** F **7.** F **8.** F **9.** F **10.** T

E. **1.** influence **2.** strictly (faithfully, religiously) **3.** burial **4.** sin **5.** celebrate **6.** attends **7.** grave **8.** God

F. **1.** F **2.** F **3.** F **4.** T **5.** F **6.** T **7.** T **8.** F

Unit 23

C. **1.** f **2.** c **3.** a **4.** h **5.** e **6.** b **7.** f **8.** d

D. **1.** e **2.** g **3.** a **4.** c **5.** b **6.** d **7.** f

E. **1.** F **2.** T **3.** T **4.** F **5.** F **6.** T **7.** T **8.** T **9.** F **10.** F

F. **1.** chance **2.** pupil **3.** definition **4.** academic (scholarly) **5.** behind
6. line **7.** inside (behind) **8.** athletic **9.** then **10.** smart **11.** club
12. scholar **13.** mind **14.** kind

G. **1.** F **2.** T **3.** F **4.** T **5.** F **6.** tuition, dormitory, and other costs
7. government, community, and university **8.** complete an application; take
an examination; write an essay; state activities, interests, memberships, and
achievements **9.** students who have good grades; athletes **10.** They provide a
chance to pay for a good education.

Unit 24

C. **1.** F **2.** T **3.** T **4.** F **5.** F **6.** T **7.** T **8.** F **9.** T **10.** T

D. **1.** announced; strike **2.** career **3.** initially **4.** luck **5.** independent
6. supports **7.** dismissed **8.** eager **9.** sudden

E. **1.** a sudden dismissal of a group of workers **2.** warning **3.** unlucky **4.** the
strike was hurting their business **5.** approval

Unit 25

C. **1.** F **2.** T **3.** F **4.** T **5.** T **6.** F **7.** T **8.** F **9.** F **10.** T

D. **1.** factor **2.** periods **3.** otherwise **4.** ordinary **5.** request **6.** unless
7. goods **8.** slightly **9.** defective **10.** wiser

E. **1.** suicide **2.** little **3.** sequence **4.** unusual **5.** marine **6.** casual
7. emphasis **8.** attempt

F. **1.** three years ago **2.** business, with a specialty in international banking
3. an import company **4.** He liked the idea of travelling to foreign countries
to buy things that he could sell at home. **5.** Andy had hardly any practical
experience. **6.** the factors that cause inflation **7.** dealing with defective
goods, angry customers **8.** Yes. $135,000 **9.** expand it **10.** if inflation
continues to rise

Words Assumed for Volume 1

a	at	book	clean	difficult
able	August	born	clock	dinner
about	aunt	both	clothes	dirty
absent		box	clothing	do
after		boy	coat	doctor
again	baby	bread	coffee	dog
age	bad	breakfast	cold	dollar
ago	ball	bring	color	door
air	bank	brother	come	dormitory
all	bath	brown	complete	down
almost	be (am, is,	build	continue	dream
already	are, was,	(built)	cook	drink
also	were, been)	busy	corner	drive
always	beautiful	but	correct	during
an	because	buy	cost	
and	become	(bought)	could	
animal	bed	by	country	each
another	before		cousin	ear
answer	begin		cow	east
any	beside	call	cry	easy
anybody	best	can	cup	eat
anyone	better	can't	cut	egg
anything	between	car		eight
anywhere	big	cat		elephant
apple	bird	centimeter	dance	eleven
April	black	chair	dark	end
are	blackboard	chicken	daughter	enough
arm	blood	child	day	enter
arms	blue	(children)	dead	etc. (etcetera)
arrive	board	church	December	every
as	boat	city	desk	explain
ask	bone	class	different	eye

February	gram	it	man (men)	no one
Friday	grandfather	its	many	(no-one)
face	grandmother	itself	map	north
fall (n)	grass		marry	nose
false	green		may	not
family		job	maybe	nothing
famous			me	now
far	hair		mean (v)	nowhere
fast	half	key	meat	number
fat	hand	kilogram	medicine	
father	handsome	kilometer	meet	
feel	happy	king	meter	ocean
feet	hat	kiss	might	o'clock
female	have	kitchen	milk	of
few	have to	knife	million	off
fifth	he	know	minute	office
find	head		mistake	often
fine	hear		money	old
finger	help	lady	month	on
finish	her	land	moon	once
fire	herself	language	more	one
first	here	large	morning	only
fish	high	last (adj)	most	open
five	him	late	mother	or
flag	himself	laugh	mountain	other
floor	his	learn	mouth	our
flower	hit	left	move	ours
fly	hold	leg	movies	ourselves
food	holiday	lesson	much	out
foot	home	letter	music	over
(feet)	hope	library	must	
forget	horse	life	my	
forth	hospital	like	myself	page
forty	hot	listen		paper
four	hotel	little		parent
free	hour	live	name	part
friend	house	long	near	party
from	how	look	necessary	past
front	hundred	a lot of	need	pay
fruit	husband	love	neighbor	peace
future		lunch	never	pen
			new	pencil
	I		news	permit
garden	ice	Miss	newspaper	person
get	idea	Mr.	next	(people)
gift	if	Mrs.	nice	picture
girl	important	machine	night	plane
give	in	magazine	nine	play
go	inside	mail	no	please
gold	interest	make	nobody	police
good	into	(made)	noise	poor
good-bye	is	male	none	practice

pretty	ship	stand	this	warm
price	shirt	start	those	wash
problem	shoe	stone	thousand	watch
put	shop	stop	three	water
	short	story	throw	way
	should	street	time	we
queen	show	strong	today	weather
question	shut	student	tomorrow	week
quiet	sick	study	tonight	well
	side	subject	too	west
	sing	such	tooth	what
radio	sister	sugar	top	when
railroad	sit	summer	train	where
rain	six	sun	tree	which
read	sleep	swim	true	white
red	slow		try	who
remember	small		twelve	whom
repeat	smile	table	twenty	why
return	snow	take	twice	wife
rice	so	talk	two	will
rich	soap	tall	type	winter
right	some	tea		with
river	somebody	teach		woman
road	somehow	telephone	umbrella	(women)
room	someone	tell	uncle	word
round	something	ten	understand	work
run	sometimes	test	university	would
	somewhere	thank	up	write
	son	the	us	wrong
sad	song	their	use	
salt	soon	them		
same	sorry	themselves		year
say	soup	then	very	yellow
school	south	therefore		yes
second	speak	these		yesterday
see	spell	they	wait	you
sell	spend	thin	wake	young
send	spoon	thing	walk	your
seven	sport	think	wall	yourself
she	spring	third	want	yourselves

In addition, the following closed sets have been assumed:

days of the week
months of the year
cardinal numbers
ordinal numbers

Words in Volume 1

Numbers refer to **volume** and unit.

accept, **1**-1
address, **1**-6
advantage, **1**-12
afternoon, **1**-15
air force, **1**-18
airplane, **1**-2
airport, **1**-2
allow, **1**-8
ambition, **1**-14
ambulance, **1**-16
apartment, **1**-3
apply, **1**-1
army, **1**-18
around, **1**-19
artist, **1**-14
assign(ment), **1**-8
attempt, **1**-1
audience, **1**-9
automobile, **1**-2

back, **1**-16
bacon, **1**-15
band, **1**-25
barn, **1**-19
baseball, **1**-10
basement, **1**-12
beach, **1**-9
beef, **1**-15
bell, **1**-8

bench, **1**-9
bicycle, **1**-11
bill, **1**-24
bleed/blood, **1**-16
blow, **1**-4
body, **1**-16
boot, **1**-17
boring, **1**-9
boss, **1**-5
bowl, **1**-15
break, **1**-16
brick, **1**-12
bridge, **1**-11
bus, **1**-2
business, **1**-5

cafeteria, **1**-8
camera, **1**-7
camp, **1**-21
campus, **1**-8
card, **1**-21
careful/less, **1**-5
carry, **1**-7
cave, **1**-21
cent, **1**-6
chair, **1**-12
change, **1**-17
chapter, **1**-8
cheap, **1**-6

cheese, **1**-15
choose, **1**-8
clear, **1**-4
clerk, **1**-6
climb, **1**-21
coast, **1**-23
collect (call), **1**-24
college, **1**-1
comedy, **1**-25
comfortable, **1**-12
commit, **1**-22
common, **1**-16
communicate, **1**-6
company, **1**-5
compete, **1**-10
complete, **1**-1
concert, **1**-9
contract, **1**-14
cool, **1**-21
corn, **1**-19
cost, **1**-21
course, **1**-8
crime, **1**-22
cross, **1**-11
crowd, **1**-10

date, **1**-21
decide, **1**-3
declare, **1**-20

deep/depth, **1**-23
deliver, **1**-6
dial, **1**-24
direction, **1**-21
dissappear, **1**-22
distance (long), **1**-24
dormitory, **1**-1
dress, **1**-17
dry, **1**-4
dull, **1**-25

early, **1**-4
earth, **1**-23
edge, **1**-11
electricity, **1**-3
elementary school, **1**-1
else, **1**-25
embassy/ambassador, **1**-20
emergency, **1**-24
employ(ee), **1**-5
empty, **1**-2
enemy, **1**-18
enjoy, **1**-7
entertainment, **1**-9
envelope, **1**-6
ever, **1**-21
examine, **1**-16
excited, **1**-7
excuse, **1**-16
expensive, **1**-6
experience, **1**-14

factory, **1**-5
fan, **1**-10
fan, **1**-23
farm, **1**-19
fear, **1**-22
fence, **1**-19
fever, **1**-16
field, **1**-19
fight, **1**-18
film, **1**-25
finally, **1**-13
fog, **1**-23
forbid, **1**-20
force, **1**-20
forecast, **1**-4
foreign, **1**-6
fork, **1**-15
fortunately, **1**-14

frequent, **1**-24
fresh, **1**-15
frighten, **1**-18
fun, **1**-25
funny, **1**-9
furniture, **1**-3

game, **1**-10
garage, **1**-12
gas, **1**-12
geography, **1**-23
glad, **1**-7
glass, **1**-15
gloves, **1**-17
golf, **1**-9
government, **1**-20
grade, **1**-8
graduate, **1**-1
ground, **1**-23
group, **1**-10
grow, **1**-19
guard, **1**-18
guess, **1**-13
guest, **1**-12
gun, **1**-18

handle, **1**-20
hang up, **1**-24
hard, **1**-23
hate, **1**-22
head, **1**-20
health, **1**-16
heat, **1**-12
heavy, **1**-13
helicopter, **1**-18
high school, **1**-1
hill, **1**-23
hobby, **1**-9
honest/honor, **1**-20
horn, **1**-11
horrible, **1**-18
hurry, **1**-11
hurt, **1**-16

ill, **1**-16
impersonal, **1**-24
indoors, **1**-10
insect, **1**-21
instrument, **1**-24

insure, **1**-13
intersection, **1**-11
interview, **1**-5
invitation, **1**-13
item, **1**-13

jacket, **1**-17
jail, **1**-22
joke, **1**-25
juice, **1**-15
jungle, **1**-23

kill, **1**-18

landlord/lady, **1**-3
lane, **1**-11
last (v), **1**-7
lawn, **1**-12
lawyer, **1**-14
lease, **1**-12
leather, **1**-17
leave, **1**-7
license, **1**-14
light, **1**-13
light, **1**-3
limit, **1**-13
lobby, **1**-21
local, **1**-24
lose/loss, **1**-10
low, **1**-14
luggage, **1**-7

maid, **1**-14
message, **1**-24
middle, **1**-11
midnight, **1**-22
military, **1**-18
mirror, **1**-17
motel, **1**-7
move, **1**-11
mud, **1**-23
murder, **1**-22
mystery, **1**-22

navy, **1**-18
neighborhood, **1**-3
noon, **1**-8
nurse, **1**-14

odd, 1-25
operator, 1-24
opinion, 1-20
orchestra, 1-9
ounce, 1-13
outdoors, 1-10
outside, 1-6
overnight, 1-7
overseas, 1-6

package, 1-13
pain, 1-16
pair, 1-17
parade, 1-18
park (n), 1-9
park (v), 1-2
pay(ment), 1-5
personality, 1-25
photography, 1-7
piano, 1-9
picnic, 1-21
piece, 1-15
pig, 1-15
pill, 1-16
place, 1-3
plan, 1-14
plant, 1-19
plate, 1-15
play (drama), 1-25
pocket, 1-17
pool, 1-25
pork, 1-15
postage, 1-6
postcard, 1-6
pound, 1-13
president, 1-20
prevent, 1-21
prince, 1-20
prize, 1-10
profession, 1-14
professor, 1-8
program, 1-9
promise, 1-20
proof, 1-22
purchase, 1-13
purse, 1-22
push, 1-11
puzzle, 1-25

raise, 1-19
ranch, 1-19
rarely, 1-13
reach, 1-11
receive, 1-5
recreation, 1-9
rent, 1-3
reply to, 1-13
require, 1-8
respect, 1-14
restaurant, 1-15
ride, 1-19
ring (v), 1-8
roommate, 1-1

sandwich, 1-15
scale, 1-13
schedule, 1-8
sea, 1-23
seal, 1-13
search, 1-3
secretary, 1-5
servant, 1-14
sheep, 1-19
shine, 1-4
shoot, 1-22
shore, 1-23
shout, 1-22
shy, 1-25
side, 1-11
skill, 1-14
skirt, 1-17
sky, 1-4
soldier, 1-18
space, 1-12
speech, 1-20
stamp, 1-6
station, 1-2
stay, 1-7
steal, 1-22
stomach, 1-16
store/storage, 1-12
storm, 1-4
strange, 1-23
suburb, 1-12
succeed, 1-10
suitcase, 1-21
surprise, 1-24

taxi, 1-11
team, 1-10
tears, 1-25
television, 1-9
tennis, 1-10
ticket, 1-2
tie, 1-17
tourist, 1-21
traffic, 1-2
transportation, 1-2
travel, 1-7
trick, 1-25
trip, 1-2
trouble, 1-20
trust, 1-20
tuition, 1-8
turn, 1-11

ugly, 1-17
unfortunately, 1-14
unfurnished, 1-3
useful, 1-19
usually/unusual, 1-4
utilities, 1-12

vacation, 1-7
valley, 1-19
vegetable, 1-19
visit, 1-7
voice, 1-24

wallet, 1-22
war, 1-18
wave, 1-23
weak, 1-10
wear, 1-17
weigh/weight, 1-13
wheat, 1-19
wheel, 1-11
win, 1-10
wind, 1-4
window, 1-6
without, 1-17
wool, 1-17
worry, 1-8

Words in Volume 2

Numbers refer to **volume** and unit.

Index

Words in Volume 3

Numbers refer to **volume** and unit.